Henry Garland

Galatians in the Greek New Testament

Books by KENNETH S. WUEST . . .

Golden Nuggets in the Greek New Testament
Bypaths in the Greek New Testament
Treasures from the Greek New Testament
Untranslatable Riches from the Greek New Testament
Philippians in the Greek New Testament
First Peter in the Greek New Testament
Galatians in the Greek New Testament
Studies in the Vocabulary of the Greek New Testament

Galatians in the Greek New Testament

For the English Reader

by
KENNETH S. WUEST

Second Edition

WM. B. EERDMANS PUBLISHING COMPANY
Grand Rapids   1946   Michigan

GALATIANS
Copyright, 1944
by KENNETH S. WUEST

All Rights Reserved.

PRINTED IN THE UNITED STATES OF AMERICA

DEDICATED

To John C. Page, D.D., my honored and beloved instructor in Bible Doctrine and Homiletics during student days at the Moody Bible Institute, whose masterful teaching technique, clear exposition of the Word, and humble Christian life redolent with the fragrance of the Lord Jesus, have left their deep impression upon my life and ministry.

Preface

The story of this book can be summed up in the following words: "Other men have labored. The author has entered into their labors." Whatever original work the writer has done, concerns itself chiefly with the ministry of the Holy Spirit and its relationship to the spiritual situation in the Galatian churches at the time of the inroads of the Judaizers, a theme which the commentaries do not treat adequately. Seven authorities on the Greek New Testament were consulted as the writer studied the words, phrases, and sentences of the text, and others were brought in when needed. Where portions are quoted verbatim, due recognition has been given the particular author, but the writer has for the most part made the material his own, and has put it in words which the average Bible student can understand. The seven authorities in their alphabetical order are: Henry Alford, *The Greek Testament;* Ernest DeWitt Burton, *A Critical and Exegetical Commentary on St. Paul's Epistle to the Galatians;* Bishop J. B. Lightfoot, *Saint Paul's Epistle to the Galatians;* Heinrich Meyer, *Critical and Exegetical Commentary on the New Testament;* Frederic Rendall in *Expositor's Greek Testament;* A. T. Robertson, *Word Pictures in the New Testament,* and Marvin R. Vincent, *Word Studies in the New Testament.* The supplementary authorities are: Joseph H. Thayer, *Greek-English Lexicon of the New Testament;* James Hope Moulton and George Milligan, *Vocabulary of the Greek Testament;* Herman Cremer, *Biblico-Theological Lexicon of New Testament Greek;* Liddel and Scott, *Greek-English Lexicon* (classical); Archbishop Trench, *New Testament Synonyms;* H. E. Dana, and Julius R. Mantey, *A Manual Grammar of the Greek New Testament;* Henry C. Thiessen, *Introduction to the New Testament,* and Theodor Zahn, *Introduction to the New Testament.*

The writer has made available to the student of the English Bible, a wealth of interpretive and translation material from these authorities to which he otherwise would have no access (with the exception of Robertson's *Word Pictures*), and he has tried to present it in language which the average student is able to follow. Many of the Greek words commented upon have been included in their transliterated form for those who are conversant with the Greek New Testament.

This is no book to peruse in one's easy chair. It is designed like its predecessors, *Philippians in the Greek New Testament,* and *First Peter in the Greek New Testament,* for use on the Christian's study table alongside of his Bible. The book is a simplified commentary on the Greek text of Galatians, making available to the Bible student who is not acquainted with Greek, and who has had no formal training in Bible study, a wealth of informative and explanatory material that will throw a flood of light upon his English Bible. The translation offered is what might be called a fuller translation, using more words than a standard version of the Scriptures in order to bring out more of the richness of the Greek, and make certain passages clearer, where the condensed literality of the standard translations tends to obscure their meaning. Words in parenthesis are not part of the translation but are explanatory. The translation must not be used as a substitute for, but as a companion to the standard translation the student is using.

The book is not written for the scholar, and lays no claim to being a finished piece of work on the Greek text of Galatians. It is designed for those who love the Lord and His Word and delight in feasting upon it. The index makes it possible for the student to turn quickly to any verse desired. Where a word or subject is treated more fully or in its every New Testament occurrence in the author's other books, a footnote will direct the reader to the page or pages where that treatment may be found. The English translation referred to is the Authorized Version. The Greek text used is Nestle's. K. S. W.

CONTENTS

1 The Historical Background of the Letter 11

2 The Analysis of the Letter 24

3 The Exegesis of the Letter 28

4 The Complete Letter in a Fuller Translation 181

1

The Historical Background of the Letter

Before entering upon an exegetical study of Paul's Galatian letter, we must consider the following questions: first, *Where were the Galatian churches located?*; second, *Who were the Galatians?*; and third, *Who were the Judaizers and what did they teach?*

First, then, as to the location of the Galatian churches. Some have held that these churches were situated in that section of Asia Minor designated on the map as Galatia, in which are situated the cities of Pessinus, Ancyra, and Tavium. This is known as the North Galatian theory. Others hold that these churches were located in the cities of Pisidian Antioch,[1] Iconium, Lystra, and Derbe. This is the South Galatian theory. The first theory had a clear field until Sir William M. Ramsay, a traveller in Asia Minor and a student of the Book of Acts, demonstrated that the Roman province of Galatia included at the time of the founding of the Galatian churches, not only the territory of Galatia, but also the country immediately to the south of it in which were situated the cities of Pisidian Antioch, Iconium, Lystra, and Derbe.

In 278-277 B.C., a people known as the Gauls left their home in southern Europe and settled in northern Asia Minor. After 232 B.C., their state became known as Galatia. King Amyntas (35-25 B.C.), the last independent ruler of Galatia, bequeathed his kingdom to Rome, and Galatia became a Roman province, 25 B.C. During the first century, the term *Galatia* was used in two different senses: *geographically*, it referred to the territory

---

1. We must distinguish between the city of Antioch in Syria, and the city of the same name in Pisidia.

in the northern part of the central plateau of Asia Minor where the Gauls lived; and *politically,* it was used to designate the Roman province of Galatia as it varied in extent. There was a wide difference between North and South Galatia in respect to language, occupation, nationality, and social organization. The northern section was still mainly populated by the Gauls, and was pastoral, with comparatively little commerce and few roads.

But in South Galatia the situation was radically different. This section was full of flourishing cities, and was enriched by the constant flow of commerce across it. This was the natural result of its geographical position and political history. In ancient times it was the highway along which Asiatic monarchs kept up their communications with the western coast of Asia Minor. When Greek monarchs ruled in Syria and Asia Minor, the highway between their capitals, Syrian Antioch and Ephesus, passed through South Galatia, and was the principal channel through which Greek civilization flowed eastward. These monarchs planted colonies of Jews and Greeks along the extent of this highway. The Caesars inherited the policy of the Greek monarchs, and planted fresh colonies along this road in order to secure this important route to the east for their legions and their commerce.

Dr. Henry Clarence Thiessen, B.D., Ph.D., D.D., chairman of the Department of Bible, Theology, and Philosophy at Wheaton College, Wheaton, Illinois, an authority among evangelical scholars, says in his most excellent book, *Introduction to the New Testament,* that now all scholars agree that Paul was in the province of Galatia when he on his first missionary journey visited Antioch, Iconium, Lystra, and Derbe (Acts 13:1-14:28). He says that Sir William Ramsay has proved this conclusively, and that no one today disputes the assertion. Dr. Thiessen also states that it seems clear that Paul on his second missionary journey (Acts 15:36-18:22) went through North Galatia (Acts 16:6) after he had passed through South Galatia, Luke using the term *Galatian* in its territorial sense. On his third journey, he visited the disciples in North Galatia made on the second journey (Acts 18:23). Dr. Thiessen remarks that it is significant that

Luke uses the word *disciples* rather than *churches* in connection with Paul's visit to North Galatia on his third journey. The implication is clear that the Galatian churches as such were in South Galatia and that there were only scattered disciples in the north section. Paul, Dr. Thiessen says, always used the provincial names of the districts that were under the Roman domination, never the territorial, except as the two were identical in significance. He speaks of Achaia, Macedonia, Illyricum, Dalmatia, Judaea (in the Roman sense of Palestine), Arabia, and Asia as provinces.

Dr. Thiessen asks some significant questions, the obvious answers to which point to the opinion that, as he says, the Galatian letter was written primarily to the churches of Pisidian Antioch, Iconium, Lystra, and Derbe. First, *is it likely since Paul always used the provincial names of districts, that he would speak of Galatia in any other sense? Second, would it not be strange for Luke to tell us so much about the founding of churches in South Galatia (Acts 13:14-14:23), and for Paul to say nothing about them? Third, does it not seem strange, on the other hand, to think that Paul would write so weighty a letter as the Epistle to the Galatians to churches whose founding is practically passed over in silence by Luke, as would be the case if the Galatian churches were located in North Galatia? Fourth, would it not be strange also for the Judaizers of Palestine to pass by the most important cities of Iconium and Antioch in South Galatia, where there were a good many Jews, and no doubt, some Jewish Christians, and go to the remoter Galatian country to do their mischievous work?*

The location of the Galatian churches in South Galatia, will help us understand the identity of the Galatian Christians. And this brings us to our next question, *Who were the Galatians?* It was Paul's practice to establish groups of churches around the capitals of the Roman provinces, link those centers together by chains of churches along the principal roads, and so bring into being an ecclesiastical organization closely corresponding to the divisions of the Roman empire. He made the provincial capitals of Pisidian Antioch, Corinth, and Ephesus, the centers of church life, as they were centers of imperial administration, and surrounded each with its group of dependent churches. Paul and Barnabas left Syrian Antioch on their first missionary journey with the purpose of extending the gospel to the Greek cities of Asia Minor and the famous centers of Greek civilization in Greece itself. This was a radical departure from the previous method by which the gospel was spread. Heretofore, the good news was spread by providential circumstances such as persecution, where refugees took their faith with them in their flight (Acts 8:1-4). But here we have a purely missionary enterprize. They sailed to Cyprus, landed at Salamis, went through the island, took a boat at Paphos and sailed to Perga, and then took the highway to Pisidian Antioch. This highway continued to Ephesus, which city would put them in touch with the Greek cities of Asia Minor and the mainland of Greece itself. Paul could have gone to Ephesus by sea from Perga, but at a certain time of the year, autumn, the violence of the winds made the sea voyage along the Aegean coast dangerous, and travellers would take the highway from Perga through Antioch. Had Paul intended to evangelize the cities of South Galatia, he would have taken the overland route from Syrian Antioch through Tarsus, as he did on his second journey.

Arriving at Antioch, he was seized with a sudden attack of illness which forced him to stay in that city, and made necessary the abandonment of his projected tour of evangelism in the Greek cities of Asia Minor and the Greek mainland (Gal. 4:13). There in Antioch he preached the gospel and from there he was driven by the Jews. He could not continue his journey westward to Ephesus because of his illness, so the only thing he could do was to strike out for home. He accordingly took the great highway back through Tarsus on which the cities of Iconium, Lystra, and Derbe were located. After establishing churches in these cities, instead of going back to Syrian Antioch by way of Tarsus, he retraced his steps in order to establish his young converts in the Faith, his illness having been presumably alleviated, which fact permitted him to take the long way home.

The religion of the Gentiles in the South Galatian cities was more oriental than Greek. Its degraded type of sensuous worship could hardly satisfy the conscience even of a heathen community to which the influences of western civilization had come. Greek philosophy and Roman morality created a nobler idea of human duty and divine government than could be reconciled with the popular religion. Thus all the better feelings of educated men and women were stirred to revolt against the degraded superstition of the masses.

Into this conflict of religious ideas, the Jewish synagogue entered. The Gentiles flocked to its higher and nobler conceptions. However, while they gave adherence to the exalted ethics of the synagogue, yet they would have nothing to do with the sacrificial system which centered in the Jerusalem Temple. To Paul's preaching, they gave a cordial welcome.

In the synagogue at Antioch (Acts 13:14-43), the Jews heard the impotence of the law for salvation announced, and the Gentiles heard the offer of a salvation procured at the Cross and given in answer to faith in Christ alone. From that hour, both Jew and Gentile recognized in Paul the foremost champion of the Gentiles, and the most formidable adversary of Judaism, which latter had been set aside by God at the Cross, but which, under an apostate priesthood, was still being nominally observed.

Before this first missionary journey, the Christian churches had been predominately Jewish. The teachers were Jewish with an Old Testament background. While interpreting the Old Testament in a new light, they yet fixed their hopes on the future kingdom of a national Messiah. But now, the newly formed churches were predominately Gentile, and the Gentiles recognized the Lord Jesus, not as a Saviour looked upon as the Messiah of Israel only, but as a world-Saviour. Thus, the Galatian Christians were not for the most part, the fickle-minded Gauls of North Galatia, but Greeks and Jews of flourishing cities situated on the highways of commerce and government.

This brings us to our third question, *Who were the Judaizers, and what did they teach?* In order to answer this question properly, we must go back to Cain, for it was he who first exhibited the tendencies which form the background of the teachings and activities of the Judaizers. Adam had instructed his sons, Cain and Abel, as to the proper approach of a sinner to a holy God, namely, by means of a blood sacrifice which pointed to and symbolized the actual sacrifice for sin which God would some day set forth, even the Lord Jesus. However, the offering of such a blood sacrifice in itself would not result in the salvation of the offerer. That offering was to be only an outward visible manifestation of an inward fact, namely, the act of that offerer in placing his faith in the coming virgin-born child who would crush the head of the serpent, Satan. Without that act of faith, the offering of the sacrifice would be a mere form, and a mockery in the eyes of God.

Cain's reaction to this instruction was that he rejected the teaching of salvation through faith in a substitutionary sacrifice, and substituted for it his own personal merit and good works. Abel followed the instructions of his father, his faith leaped the centuries to the Cross, and he was declared righteous. Since the time of these two men, these two diametrically opposed tendencies are seen in the human race. We see them in the history of Israel. There always was the remnant in Israel, a little group which offered the symbolic sacrifices as an indication of a real living faith in the future substitutionary sacrifice, and there was always the larger group, which, while it went through the ritual of the Levitical sacrifices, yet exercised no heart faith to appropriate a salvation offered in grace on the basis of justice satisfied by the atonement, but depended upon personal merit and good works for salvation. These two groups were in existence in Israel in the first century. An illustration of the first is found in such believers as Zacharias, Elizabeth, Mary the virgin, the disciples other than Judas. An illustration of the second we find in the priests, Pharisees, Sadducees, and the Herodians, who while observing the sacrificial ritual of the Temple yet ignored its significance and depended for salvation upon personal merit and their own good works.

From this latter group came two attacks against New Testament truth, inspired by Satan, two attempts of the Adversary to destroy the newly-formed Christian Church. One of these was the attempt to substitute good works for faith in Christ. This was met by the letter to the Galatians. The other was the attempt to invalidate the atoning worth of the Cross by urging the Jewish wing of the Church to return to the Levitical ritual of the Temple. This was met by the Book of Hebrews.[2] The first was aimed at the Gentile wing of the Church, the second, at the Jewish group in the Church. The Judaizers were members of this unsaved group in Israel, seeking to maintain a corrupt form of the Jewish national religion as against the Christian Church which had been formed at Pentecost. So much for their identity. We now approach the question as to their teachings.

Our first source of information is Philippians 3:2-6,[3] where Paul warns the Philippian saints against the Judaizers. He calls them dogs. The Greek word was a term of reproach among both Greeks and Jews. He calls them evil workers. The term implies, not merely evil doers, but those who actually wrought against the gospel. He speaks of them as the concision. The Greek word occurs only here in the New Testament. A kindred verb is used in the Greek translation of the Old Testament, speaking of the mutilations forbidden by the Mosaic law such as the pagans were wont to inflict upon themselves in their religious rites. The Greek word which Paul uses is a play upon the Greek word *circumcision*. Paul characterizes those who were not of the true circumcision as merely mutilated. Heathen priests mutilated their own bodies. The Judaizers mutilated the message of the gospel by substituting works for grace, and thus their own lives and those of their converts.

Then Paul contrasts true believers with the Judaizers by saying that the former worship God in the Spirit whereas the latter have confidence in the flesh. The best Greek texts read, "worship by the Spirit of God." The implication is clear that the Judaizers did not worship in the energy of the Holy Spirit, which means that they were unsaved. The words *have confidence* are in the Greek literally, "have come to a settled persuasion." That is,

---
2. *Riches*, pp. 44-73.
3. *Philippians*, pp. 87-89.

these Judaizers had come to a settled belief in the merit of human attainment. They depended upon good works for acceptance with God, which teaching goes right back to Cain.

Then Paul enumerates some of the human attainments and merits which the Judaizers were depending upon for acceptance with God. The *first* was circumcision, marking out that person as a member of the Chosen People, Israel, separating the people of that nation from all other peoples as the chosen channel through which God would reveal Himself and His salvation to the human race. The rite had nothing to do with the personal salvation of a Jew or his acceptance before God. The Judaizers made it a prerequisite to salvation. Luke records the fact that "Certain men which came down from Judaea (to Antioch) taught the brethren, and said, Except ye be circumcised after the manner of Moses, ye cannot be saved" (Acts 15:1). Circumcision was obedience to a command of God. Thus it is included in what we call good works. All of which means that the Judaizers taught that salvation is by good works.

Second, they taught that acceptance with God was brought about by virtue of the fact that one was a member of the nation Israel, "of the stock of Israel." John the Baptist met this teaching when the Pharisees and Sadducees came to him. He said to them, "Think not to say within yourselves, We have Abraham to our father" (Matt. 3:9). Our Lord encountered the same teaching when the Jews claimed to have Abraham as their father, which fact would provide for their acceptance with God (John 8:39).

Third, they taught that an ecclesiastical position in the religious system of Israel gave one acceptance with God. Paul says that he could also have claimed that as a Pharisee he was accepted with God. *Fourth,* the faithful observance of the law would provide for them a righteousness acceptable with God. Paul speaks of this same thing in Romans 9:30-10:3, where Israel is said to have failed in obtaining a righteousness acceptable with God because the nation ignored the righteousness of God, Christ, given in answer to faith, and went about to establish its own righteousness by doing good works. This was typical of the rank and file of Israel, of course, with the exception of the remnant. Isaiah (64:6) speaks of the same tendency of Israel all down the ages when he predicts that at the Second Advent of Messiah, Israel will finally acknowledge that all of its righteousnesses are as filthy rags in God's sight.

Paul distinguishes between the righteousness which is in the law and the righteousness which is by faith (Rom. 10:5, 6). The first would be possible to a perfect sinless person. By his perfect obedience to God, he could accrue to himself a righteousness. But no sinner can perfectly obey the legal enactments of the Mosaic law, and therefore any attempt to produce a righteousness would result in what Isaiah calls *filthy rags*. The Judaizers clothed themselves with these. The righteousness of God, Christ, offered to the believing sinner in answer to his faith, is infinitely more precious and meritorious than any righteousness which a sinless person could accrue to himself by a perfect obedience to the will of God. Paul in Philippians 3:9,[4] says that he will have nothing to do with the righteousness which the Judaizers have. He will have nothing else but the righteousness of God.

After enumerating the various things that the Judaizers were depending upon for salvation, and saying that he could depend upon those also, Paul says that he has discarded all dependence upon these, for dependence upon these kept him from Christ. That means that the Judaizers, depending upon these things, were unsaved.

Our next source of information regarding the Judaizers we will find in Romans 2:17-3:8. Paul, writing to the believers at Rome, finds it necessary to combat this same Jewish tendency of dependence upon Jewish ancestry, the law and a knowledge of the same, and circumcision. He shows the Jew that with all his boasted privileges, he is still an unsaved man as shown by the fact that he does not practice what he preaches (2:21-24). He devotes chapter 4 to showing that salvation is not by works (1-8), not by ordinances (9-12), and not by law observance (13-25), saying that Abraham was justified by faith alone, was saved before

---

4. *Philippians*, pp. 92-98.

the rite of circumcision was performed, and that the law is a ministry of condemnation rather than of salvation.

We turn now to Philippians 1:14-18.[5] Paul is writing from his prison in Rome. He informs the Philippians that one result of his imprisonment was that many of the brethren were becoming more confident in the Lord by reason of his own fearless example, and were preaching the gospel in the face of opposition and persecution. This group, composed of true believers, was motivated by a love for Paul and sympathy for him in his present distress. The other group was announcing the Messiah out of a spirit of rivalry and envy, seeking to make Paul's imprisonment more distressing to him. They announced Messiah not sincerely, but with mixed motives, insincerely. This group was at odds with Paul. They were the Judaizers who dogged Paul's footsteps, ever seeking to undermine his work of evangelization and the founding of churches. They announced Jesus of Nazareth as Messiah, but in a most inadequate way. They could not have announced Him as the Lamb of God who took away the sins of the world, for they preached salvation by works. An illustration of the hazy, inadequate, and erroneous conception which the apostate Jewish world had of its Messiah in the first century is found in the fact that the writer to the Hebrews, in combating the Judaistic attack upon Christianity from the standpoint of a return to the Levitical sacrifices, finds it necessary to prove from Old Testament scripture that the Messiah is better than the prophets of Israel, the angels of God, superior to Moses, Joshua, and Aaron. The writer to the Hebrews was not fighting a straw man. He would not waste time nor energy nor space in his treatise to refute an argument or a system of teaching that did not exist.[6]

In addition to circumcision and obedience to the precepts of the Mosaic law, the Judaizers taught that it was necessary for these Galatian Christians to keep the Jewish feasts (Gal. 4:10). They did not touch the matter of the Levitical sacrifices so far as the Gentiles were concerned, for the latter were attracted only by

---
5. *Philippians*, pp. 41, 42.
6. *Riches*, pp. 44-54.

the pure monotheism and high precepts of the Jewish synagogue, and rejected teaching regarding salvation through a substitutionary sacrifice which this symbolic system presented. And the very fact that the Judaizers left this part of the Mosaic law alone so far as the Galatian Christians were concerned, shows that they considered the Temple sacrifices a mere form, and not an essential part of the revelation of God to Moses so far as salvation was concerned.

Thus the Judaizers belong to that section of the nation Israel that was unsaved. They are to be distinguished however from the rest of their brethren after the flesh, in that they had infiltrated into the visible Christian Church, and were attempting to set up a perverted legalism built around the Mosaic economy, whereas the others rejected Jesus as Messiah, were holding aloof from the Church, and were persecuting the Jews in the Church. While giving a mental assent to the Messiahship of Jesus of Nazareth, they had at the same time a most inadequate view of that office. They taught that acceptance with God was to be had by means of personal merit obtained through the individual's good works, and that the saved individual was sanctified by observance of the legal precepts of the Mosaic law.

The Judaizers did not attempt to introduce the economy of the Old Testament into the Church, but a false view of that economy. Sinners were saved in Old Testament times by pure grace just as they are today, without any admixture of good works. Had the Judaizers believed in their hearts in the true economy of the Old Testament, they would not have been false teachers, but true believers in the Lord Jesus, for all Old Testament saints alive when Jesus came, accepted Him as Messiah and High Priest, and those who over-lived the Cross, became members of the Body of Christ at Pentecost.

Here therefore was an attempt on the part of Satan, working through Israel, to ruin the Christian Church, not by introducing Old Testament Judaism, but a false conception of the same, by going back to Cain and his system of salvation by works. Paul was the chief exponent of grace, and the apostle to the Gentiles.

It was therefore necessary to undermine, and if possible, to destroy his work.

This the Judaizers tried to do by two methods. *First,* they endeavored to depreciate Paul's apostolic position and set up the Twelve Apostles as the real interpreters of Christ in order that they might thereby discredit his authority as a teacher of grace. They argued that Paul was not one of the original Twelve, he had not listened to Christ's voice, he had not seen His face, he had not attended on Christ's ministry, and that he had not been sent out like them at His express command. Furthermore, they said that he had not received the gospel by direct revelation from Christ as had the others, but had gathered it at second-hand from the Twelve. The *second* method they used was to substitute a salvation-by-works system for the doctrine of pure grace which Paul preached. Paul therefore found it necessary to defend his apostolic authority, which he does in the first two chapters of Galatians; and to show that salvation was by grace before the Mosaic law was given, and that the coming in of the latter did not supersede nor affect the economy of grace in the least, and this he does in chapters three and four. Then, because the teachings of the Judaizers were working havoc in the lives of the Galatian Christians, he found it necessary to introduce some corrective measures emphasizing the ministry of the Holy Spirit to the Christian, which he does in chapters five and six. Thus the epistle can be summed up in three words and divided into three sections, *Personal* (1, 2), *Doctrinal* (3, 4), *Practical* (5, 6).

The inroads of the Judaizers into the Galatian churches took place during Paul's third missionary journey, for Paul had visited them again on his second journey, and at that time there were no evidences of their destructive work. It was during his third journey, when Paul was either in Macedonia or Greece, and about A.D. 55, 56 (Thiessen) that Paul received word of the serious danger which the Galatian churches were in, and recognized in that danger, a serious threat to the whole Christian system. From the following considerations, it seems probable that the way in which Paul found out about the activities of the Judaizers was that accredited representatives of the Galatian churches had come to Paul to obtain a decision on the whole matter of their teachings concerning his apostolic credentials and his gospel of pure grace without works. Paul does not seem anywhere in the Galatian epistle to be uncertain with regard to the facts and conditions among the Galatians which are presupposed and discussed by him. It is hardly possible that his information was derived solely from private sources, letters, or oral statements of individual Christians as is the case in I Corinthians 1:11, 11:18. Again, there is nothing in the letter which would lead one to think that it is an answer to a writing sent to Paul in the name and by the direction of the churches. It is much more probable that accredited representatives of the Galatian churches came to Paul, of whom he could have inquired as to the details concerning the matters which they had brought to his attention. Otherwise he could not have written this epistle without first asking for an explanation of the surprising things that were going on, or without expressing doubt as to the truthfulness of the reports that had come to him. Being assured of the facts, he proceeds to pass judgment on them. Finding it impossible to go at once to them, he writes this letter (4:20). We are now ready for the exegetical study of its contents.[7]

---

7. The reader is urged to master the contents of the historical background before commencing his study of the letter itself.

2

The Analysis of the Letter

PERSONAL

Paul defends his apostolic authority against the efforts of the Judaizers to discredit it, by proving it to be of divine origin (Ch. 1 and 2).

I. The salutation and ascription of praise. In his salutation, Paul expands his official title into a statement of his direct commission from God, thus meeting at once the attack of his opponents against his apostolic authority, and by dwelling on the work of redemption in connection with the name of Christ, he protests against their doctrinal errors (1:1-5).

II. The Galatian Christians are rebuked and the Judaizers denounced (1:6-10).

III. Paul asserts that the gospel he preaches came to him, not from man but directly from God (1:11-2:21).

1. It was a special revelation given to Paul directly from God (1:11, 12).
2. Paul's previous education could not have been responsible for his teaching of grace, for it was directly opposed to the latter (1:13, 14).
3. Paul could not have learnt the gospel from the Twelve Apostles at Jerusalem, for he kept aloof from them for some time after his conversion (1:15-17).
4. When he did go up to Jerusalem, he only saw Peter and James, only remained fifteen days, and returned without being recognized by the mass of believers (1:18-24).

GREEK NEW TESTAMENT

5. When Paul did go back to Jerusalem after some years, he was most careful to maintain his independence of the apostles there. His fellowship with them was on terms of equality. He was not indebted to them for anything (2:1-10).

6. But Paul's independence of the Twelve is not only seen in his activities at Jerusalem, but in his act of rebuking Peter at Antioch when the latter was yielding to pressure from the legalizers, and was adding law to grace, and in that way denying the fundamental of the gospel (2:11-21).

DOCTRINAL

Paul defends his doctrine of justification by faith alone without works against that of the Judaizers who taught that the works of an individual gave him acceptance with God (Ch. 3 and 4).

I. The Galatian Christians received the Holy Spirit in answer to their faith in Christ, not through obedience to law (3:1-5).

II. Abraham was justified by faith, not works. Therefore the true children of Abraham are justified in the same way (3:6-9).

III. The Judaizers taught that the law was a means of justification. Pauls shows that the law is a means of condemnation, and that it is the Lord Jesus who rescues us from its condemnation through the blood of His Cross (3:10-14).

IV. God made provision for justification to be given on the basis of faith in Jesus Christ to the Gentiles, and also the gift of the Spirit to both Jew and Gentile, doing this before the Mosaic law was given. The law therefore cannot make void that which was done by God prior to the giving of the law (3:15-18).

V. If the law was never given as a means whereby a sinner might be saved, why was it given, and for what purpose? (3:19-4:7).

1. It was given to show man that sin is not a mere following of evil impulses, but a direct violation of the laws of God (3:19-23).

2. It was given in order that, by showing the sinner that sin was an actual transgression of God's laws, he might see the necessity of faith in a substitutionary sacrifice for sin, and thus be led to put his trust in the Christ of prophecy who would in the future die for him (3:24-29).

3. It was given because the sinner was like a child in its minority, and could therefore only be dealt with in a most elementary way (4:1-7).

VI. Yet the Galatians are determined to return to their former position as minors and slaves under law (4:8-11).

VII. Paul appeals in a touching way to the Galatians to maintain their freedom from the law. He reminds them of their enthusiastic reception of him and the gospel which he preached. He tells them of his longing to be with them now in order that he might speak to them personally (4:12-20).

VIII. The history of Hagar and Sarah illustrates the present status of law and grace. As the son of the bondwoman gave place to the son of the freewoman, so law has given place to grace (4:21-31).

PRACTICAL

I. Paul exhorts the Galatians to hold fast to the freedom from law which the Lord Jesus procured for them by the blood of His Cross, and not become entangled in a legalistic system (5:1-12).

II. They have been liberated from the law by the blood of Christ. But they are not to think that this freedom gives them the liberty to sin. The reason why they have been liberated from such an elementary method of controlling the conduct of an individual, is that they might be free to live their lives on a new principle, namely, under the control of the Holy Spirit (5:13-26).

1. He warns them not to use their freedom from the law as a pretext for sinning, thus turning liberty into license, and he exhorts them instead, to govern their lives by the motivating impulse of divine love (5:13-15).

2. The subjection of the saint to the personal control of the indwelling Holy Spirit is the secret of victory over sin and of the living of a life in which divine love is the motivating impulse (5:16-26).
   a. The Holy Spirit will suppress the activities of the evil nature as the saint trusts Him to do so and cooperates with Him in His work of sanctification (5:16-21).
   b. The Holy Spirit will produce His own fruit in the life of the saint as the latter trusts Him to do that and cooperates with Him in His work of sanctification (5:22-26).

III. The Galatian saints who have not been enticed away from grace by the wiles of the Judaizers and who therefore are still living Spirit-controlled lives, are exhorted to restore their brethren who have been led astray, back to the life under grace (6:1-5).

IV. The Galatian saints who have deserted grace for law are exhorted to put themselves under the ministry of the teachers who led them into grace, and are warned that if they do not, they will reap a harvest of corruption (6:6-10).

V. Paul's final warning against the Judaizers, and his closing words (6:11-18).

3

The Exegesis of the Letter

PERSONAL

Paul defends his apostolic authority against the efforts of the Judaizers to discredit it, by proving it to be of divine origin (chapters 1 and 2).

I. *The salutation and ascription of praise.* In his salutation, Paul expands his official title into a statement of his direct commission from God, thus meeting at once the attack of his opponents against his apostolic authority; and by dwelling on the work of redemption in connection with the name of Christ, he protests against their doctrinal errors (1:1-5).

Verse one. Paul, an apostle. By the addition of the title *apostle* to his name, Paul at the very beginning of his letter, claims to be one who is divinely commissioned to preach the gospel and authorized to plant Christianity. He conceived of his apostleship as related to the Church universal, and thought of Christianity as an organic whole, not simply as isolated centers of effort and of divine appointment in relation to it. The word *apostle* is the translation of *apostolos,* a Greek word made up of *apo* "from" and *stello* "to send," thus referring to the act of sending someone on a commission to represent the sender. It was used of a messenger or an envoy who was provided with credentials. Our word *ambassador* would be a good translation. The word *apostle* as Paul uses it here does not merely refer to one who has a message to announce, but to an appointed representative with an official status who is provided with the credentials of his office.

Not. The third word in the letter stamps it as argumentative and controversial. Paul plunges at once with characteristic vigor into a discussion of the questions at issue, his apostolic authority and the divine origin of his message. Paul was a man who could say NO.

Of men. Paul is most discriminating in the use of his prepositions in this verse. *Of* is the translation of *apo,* which means *from,* and which speaks of ultimate source. His apostleship did not come from men as its ultimate source. By the use of this preposition, he distinguishes himself from the false apostles who did not derive their commissions from God. He denies that his apostleship had a human source. The word for *men* used here, *anthropos,* the racial term, not *aner,* the individual man, emphasizes again that the source of his apostleship was not human but divine in character.

Neither by man. Neither is from *oude,* literally *not even.* Not only does Paul say that his apostleship did not find its ultimate source in mankind, but it did not find its intermediate source in man. Man was not even the agent of God in conferring that apostleship. *By* is the translation of *dia,* the preposition denoting intermediate agency. It denotes the means or instrument in the hands of an individual by which an act is performed. Thus Paul not only denies that he was made an apostle by men, but also that God used the intermediate agency of man to constitute him an apostle. His apostleship was not derived from a human source or given through a human channel. The reason why Paul changes from the plural word *men* to the singular word *man,* is that titles and offices which emanate from a body of men are conferred by their single representative. The acts of the Roman senate took effect through the reigning monarch, those of the Sanhedrin, through the high priest.

But by Jesus Christ.[1] *But* is from *alla,* the stronger of the two adversatives, *de* being the milder one. Paul is very strong in his language when contrasting the divine origin of his apostleship with the human origin of the apostleship of the false apostles. *By* is from *dia,* the preposition denoting intermediate agency. The use of *dia* here rather than *apo* indicates that Paul is speak-

---
1. *Nuggets,* pp. 111-113.

ing, not of a source of his apostleship between which and himself there intervenes an agent, but of the channel through which it came to him or of its immediate source. *Dia* when used of personal agency sometimes expresses mediate agency which is both the agent and the source itself. Here Jesus Christ is both.

And God the Father. The addition of the words *God the Father* to the name *Jesus Christ,* shows that Paul is not thinking simply of the agency through which his apostleship came to him, but also of the source through which, being ultimate, there can be no higher. Then again, both names are governed by the one preposition *dia,* showing that Jesus Christ and God the Father are not separated in his mind as sustaining different relationships to his apostleship, but are conceived of jointly, and as sustaining one relation. Taken together, therefore, the whole expression has the meaning, "directly from Jesus Christ and God the Father." Had he thought of Christ as the agent and the Father as the source, he would have used *dia* and *apo,* the prepositions of intermediate agency and of ultimate source respectively. If he had used *apo* with both names, that would have left open the possibility of a human channel. Paul received his commission as an apostle directly from the Lord Jesus when he met Him on the Damascus road (Acts 9:3-8). He offers the fact that he has seen the Lord Jesus, as a token of his apostleship (I Cor. 9:1). The open investiture may have taken place later (Acts 9:15-17; 13:2, 3). The intervention of the prophets and the Antioch church may have given a coloring to the false representations of the Judaizers that he was an apostle of men.

Who raised Him from the dead. By adding this qualifying phrase, Paul emphasizes the fact that whereas the other apostles were commissioned by the Lord Jesus while He was in His humiliation, he himself was given his commission by the resurrected glorified Christ.

Translation. *Paul an apostle, not from man (as an ultimate source), nor even through the intermediate agency of a man, but through the direct agency of Jesus Christ and God the Father, the One who raised Him out from among the dead.*

Verse two. And all the brethren which are with me. Salutations at the end of a letter, expressive of love, good-will, sympathy, and interest are from persons whose names are mentioned at the close of the letter. But persons who join in the address prefixed to a letter, are persons whose authorization is required and conveyed in it. They are indicated as joint-authors. The letter, though composed by Paul, is a letter of Paul and those named with him. These all stamp with authority what is said in the letter. Accordingly, where Paul associates anyone with himself in the prefatory superscription of his letters, it is always some person who stands in a position of authority and influence towards those addressed. The above expression could hardly refer to the Christian brethren in the churches where Paul may have been at the time of the writing of Galatians, but would more naturally refer to his fellow-travellers. In Philippians 4:21, 22, he makes a distinction between the saints resident at Rome and "the brethren which are with me." The omission of their names shows that the Galatians must have known who they were. Paul mentions them to show the Galatians that he is not alone in his doctrine of grace. The word *all* would indicate that there was a considerable number of his colleagues in the gospel ministry with him at the time.

Unto the churches of Galatia. The abruptness of the language is remarkable. In Paul's other letters, he always has a word of commendation for the churches to which he is writing, even in the case of the church at Corinth which he was taking severely to task because of serious disorders within its membership. He does not even address them as saints, although they were. This shows the extent and seriousness of their defection, also the troubled state of the apostle's mind mingled with his indignation at the actions of his converts.

The word *church* is the translation of *ekklesia,* a word akin to the verb *ekkaleo* which refers to the act of calling out a group of individuals to an assembly. The word in classical Greek referred to a summoned assembly, for instance, an assembly summoned for legislative business. In the New Testament, it refers usually to a local assembly of Christians, less frequently to the whole body of Christians as in the Ephesian letter.

Translation. *And all the brethren with me, to the assemblies of Galatia.*

Verse three. The salutation proper as given in this verse is the uniform one found in all of the Pauline church letters, but it has special significance in the Galatian letter since the recipients were turning away from the doctrine of grace toward the legalistic teachings of the Judaizers. The grace spoken of here is sanctifying grace, the enabling ministry of the Holy Spirit in the lives of the saints. The Galatian letter reveals the fact that the Galatian saints were being deprived of the ministry of the Spirit by the teaching of the Judaizers to the effect that growth in the Christian life was to be had by obedience to the legal enactments of the Mosaic law (4:19), and thus coming under the Mosaic economy in which there was no provision for an indwelling Spirit whose ministry it was to sanctify the believer, they substituted self-effort for their former dependence upon the Spirit. The salutation therefore is the outbreathing of a Pauline prayer that the Galatians might again become recipients of the full work of the Spirit in their lives. The peace here mentioned is heart peace which is the result of the ministry of the Spirit.

The names of *God the Father* and the *Lord Jesus Christ* are governed by the one preposition of ultimate source *apo,* thus indicating that they are the joint source of grace and peace, and that they cooperate in the carrying out of the plan of man's redemption.

Translation. *Grace to you and peace from God the Father and the Lord Jesus Christ.*

Verse four. Who gave Himself for our sins. Here Paul brings to the attention of the Galatian Christians who were practically ignoring the substitutionary character of the atoning death of the Lord Jesus, a declaration of the true ground of acceptance with God (2:21; 5:4). This was purposely added because the Galatians were falling back on works as the ground of such acceptance. The voluntary aspect of the death of our Lord is brought out here. He said, "Lo, I come to do thy will, O God" (Heb. 10:9). The preposition *for* is *huper,* a word that speaks of substitution, which was its usual meaning in the secular world of the first century. The professional letter writer acting in behalf of and instead of the illiterate, would put that fact at the close of a document which he wrote, using this word; for instance, *"Heraikleios Horou; I wrote on behalf of him who does not know letters."* This is the usual formula which makes the contents legal. Two instances in the New Testament where *huper* in its substitutionary usage is as plain as in the secular documents are: John 11:50, where Caiaphas uses it to speak of a political substitution, not a theological, although John finds that too; and II Corinthians 5:14, 15 in the words *if one died for all,* that is, *instead of and in behalf of*. Thus Paul brings over against the Judaizers' bloodless religion, the doctrine of the substitutionary atonement which teaches that the Lord Jesus took our place with relation to our sins and gave Himself as the Sacrifice that would perfectly satisfy the just demands of God's holy law which the human race has violated.

That He might deliver us from this present evil world. Deliver is the translation of *exaireo* which means *to pluck out, to draw out, to rescue, to deliver.* The word strikes the keynote of the letter. The gospel is a rescue, an emanicipation from a state of bondage. The word here denotes, not a *removal* from, but a *rescue* from the power of the ethical characteristics of the present age. *World* is from *aionos* which Trench defines as follows: *"All that floating mass of thoughts, opinions, maxims, speculations, hopes, impulses, aims, aspirations, at any time current in the world, which it may be impossible to seize and accurately define, but which constitute a most real and effective power, being the moral or immoral atmosphere which at every moment of our lives we inhale, again inevitably to exhale."* It is that particular phase of human society, the one which our Lord found existing when He came the first time, which He will still find existing when He comes the second time, and which will be displaced by a new order of things in the Millennium. The word *present* is used twice elsewhere where it is applied to things existing, by way of contrast to things future (Rom. 8:38; I Cor. 3:22).

The word *evil* is not from *kakos* here but *poneros*. In the latter word, the positive activity of evil comes out far more decidedly than in the former. The *kakos* man may be content to perish in his own corruption, but the *poneros* man is not content unless he is corrupting others as well, and drawing them into the same destruction with himself. Satan is not called the *kakos one* but the *poneros one*. This present age is described by Paul as *poneros*. The English word which best translates this Greek word is *pernicious*.

Webster says, *"That is pernicious which works mischief or destruction."* This present age therefore is not content to perish in its own corruption, but seeks to drag all men with it down to its own inevitable destruction. The outstanding philosophy of religion of this present pernicious age is, that acceptance with Deity is by means of the good works of the individual. Every system of religion except that in the Bible bases salvation upon the good works of the worshipper. The Judaizers were part of this present evil age. Their system, not content with dragging down its own devotees to destruction, was attempting to pull down the Christian Church with it. Paul says that the substitutionary atonement of the Lord Jesus is that which will rescue the poor lost sinner from the clutches of the pernicious teachings of the Judaizers.

According to the will of God and our Father. But Paul hastens to add that the act of Christ rescuing us is not according to our plan, or in proportion to our legal obedience or because of any quality in us, but according to the Father's sovereign will which is the standard of all the process of redemption. This rescue therefore is according to the procedure prescribed by Him. All of which means that the salvation procured on the Cross for us by our Lord is to be received by faith aside from any merit of our own. We cannot earn what Christ procured for us. Salvation is given free, gratis, as a gift.

Translation. *Who gave Himself in behalf of our sins so that He might rescue us out from this present pernicious age, according to the will of our God and Father.*

Verse five. Translation. *To whom be the glory for ever and ever. Amen.*

II. *The Galatian Christians are rebuked and the Judaizers denounced* (1:6-10).

Verses six and seven. I marvel that you are so soon removed. *Marvel* is from *thaumazo* which means *to wonder at, to marvel.* Its cognate adjective means *wonderful, marvelous.* Thus Paul considered the defection of the Galatian Christians as an extraordinary thing. *Alford* says of this word, *"a word of mildness, inasmuch as it imports that better things were expected of them, — and of condescension, as letting down the writer to the level of the readers and even challenging explanation from them. Still, like many such mild words, it carries to the guilty conscience even sharper rebuke than a harsher one would."* *Are removed* is from *metatithemi* which means "to transpose two things, one of which is put in the place of the other." In classical Greek it was used of a turncoat. The word is used of one altering his opinion or becoming of another mind. The word was also used of desertion or revolt, frequently of a change in religion, philosophy, or morals. The present tense indicates that when Paul wrote, the defection of the Galatians was yet only in progress. Had he used the perfect tense, that would have indicated that the Galatians had actually and finally turned against grace and had come to a settled attitude in the matter. The mind of Paul wavers beween fear and hope as to the outcome. Paul was trying desperately to arrest the progress of this new doctrinal infection if he could. The Judaizers had not yet achieved any decisive success, although the Galatians were disposed to lend a ready ear to their insinuations.

So soon is from *tacheos.* The word is used also in I Timothy 5:22 where Timothy is warned against ordaining anyone as an elder in a hurried fashion. The word means "readily, rashly, quickly," and speaks here of the rapidity with which the Galatians were turning away from Paul and his teaching of grace, to the Judaizers with their teaching of works.

From him who called you into the grace of Christ. The One who called the Galatians was God. *Called* is from *kaleo*. Its distinctive use in the New Testament is to call a person for a definite purpose. Hence, it is synonymous with *to select* or *choose*. It refers to the act of calling someone so that he may hear, come, and do that which is incumbent upon him. It thus is a word that becomes a technical term for special relationships. In secular Greek it was used of a summons in the law courts. It denotes in the New Testament a call from God or in God's Name, a call to participate in the revelation of grace. Paul's use of the word in general suggests that he thought of those only as called who obeyed the divine summons. Of a rejected call he never speaks. The word *grace*[2] is in the locative of sphere. God called the Galatians in the sphere of grace. That is, when He effectually summoned them to a participation in the salvation procured by His Son on the Cross, it was on a basis, not of works, but of a salvation unmerited by them and freely bestowed, offered out of the pure generosity and love of the heart of God, with no strings tied to it, offered as a free gift to be accepted by the outstretched hand of faith. This put the Galatians in a position in relationship to God in which they were the objects of His everlasting favor. In speaking of the change of position on the part of the Galatians, it would be more natural for Paul to refer to the state in which God's call they are or should be than to emphasize the basis or instrument of God's call. The Galatians were abandoning the position of grace, the relation toward God which made them the objects of the grace of Christ and participants in its benefits, to put themselves under law which could only award them their sad desserts.

Unto another gospel; which is not another. Paul uses two Greek words, both of which mean *another,* but which have a further distinct meaning of their own. The first is *heteros,* the second *allos. Heteros* means *another of a different kind, allos,*

---

2. *Treasures,* pp. 15-19.

another of the same kind. Heteros denotes qualitative difference, *allos*, numerical difference. *Heteros* distinguishes one of two. *Allos* adds one besides. Every *heteros* is an *allos,* but not every *allos* is a *heteros. Heteros* involves the idea of difference of kind, while *allos* denotes simply distinction of individuals. *Heteros* sometimes refers however, not only to difference in kind but also speaks of the fact that the character of the thing is evil or bad. That is, the fact that something differs in kind from something else, makes that thing to be of an evil character. We have the word *heterodoxy*, made up of *heteros,* and the word *doxa* which means *opinion.* Paul's doctrine of grace is God's truth, and anything that differs in kind from it must necessarily be false doctrine. *Heterodoxy* is false doctrine.

When Paul speaks of the Galatians turning to a *heteros* gospel, he means that they are turning to a gospel that is false in its doctrine. It is not only different in character from the gospel which he preached to the Galatians, but it is different in a bad sense. It is essentially evil. We have here in the expression, *heteros gospel,* a contradiction in terms. *Gospel* is from *euaggelion* which means *good news.* There cannot be a *heteros good news,* that is, a message of good news different in kind from that which Paul preached, and different in an evil sense, and yet be a message of good news. A salvation-by-works message is no good news to a lost sinner, *first,* because the Bible says "not by works of righteousness which we have done, but according to His mercy He saved us" (Titus 3:5), and *second,* if salvation would be by good works, one would not know how many good works a person must do to be saved or after being saved, to keep saved. No one could have any assurance of acceptance with God or security in salvation from such preaching. Thus, Paul stamps the message of the Judaizers as heterodoxy, false doctrine.

Then he says that it is not an *allos* gospel. It is not only different in kind. It is not a gospel at all. It is not another gospel even when considered in a numerical way. There can be only one message of good news. *Arthur S. Way* in his excellent translation of Galatians renders *heteros gospel, an opposition gospel, allos gospel, an alternative gospel.* Thus, the Galatians were turning to an opposition gospel diametrically opposed to Paul's message of grace, and this opposition gospel was not an alternative one.

But there be some that trouble you. The word *trouble* is from *tarasso* which means "to disturb mentally" with excitement, perplexity, and fear. The present tense of this participle indicates that the Judaizers were still in Galatia at the time Paul wrote this letter, and that the Galatian letter was written to combat them while they were in the very midst of their work. The definite article is used with the participle, pointing out in a more marked manner, the notorious occupation of these men. *Some* is from *tines,* an indefinite pronoun. In the use of this word Paul refers to the Judaizers with a certain studied vagueness. They were evidently strangers whom the apostle treats with real or affected contempt.

And would pervert the gospel of Christ. The word *would* is from *thelo* which means *to desire.* It is in the present tense which indicates that the troubling was a present fact, the perversion was yet only a wish of the Judaizers, and that the Galatians had not completely succumbed to their influence. The word *pervert* is from *metastrepho* which means "to reverse, to change to the opposite, to turn about." The purpose of the Judaizers was to so change the gospel of grace which Paul preached, that it would be the reverse of what it was, a message of salvation by good works instead of a message of a salvation offered free in answer to faith. It was not merely to derange it or to turn aside its true meaning. It was to transform it into something diametrically opposed to what it was originally, into something of an opposite nature. Thus the actions of the Judaizers themselves testify to the mutual incompatibility of law and grace. These two systems have nothing in common; as Paul says, "If by grace, then is it no more of works: otherwise grace is no more grace. But if it be of works, then is it no more grace: otherwise work is no more work" (Rom. 11:6).

Translation. *I am marvelling that in such a manner suddenly, you are becoming of another mind and are deserting from Him who called you in the sphere of Christ's grace to a message of good news diametrically opposed to the gospel, which message is not another gospel of the same kind. Only there are certain ones who are troubling your minds, and are desiring to pervert the gospel of Christ.*

Verse eight. *But though we or an angel from heaven. But* is from *alla*, the stronger of two Greek adversatives. This strong language shows how serious Paul considered the differences to be between his gospel and the message of the Judaizers. He is concerned over the fact that the Galatians probably regarded the gospel he preached as, after all, not so very different from the message of the Judaizers. His own strong sense of the serious difference between the two messages, is responsible for the vehemence of his feelings in the premises. By the use of the plural pronoun *we,* Paul associates with himself his colleagues, Barnabas, Silas, and Timothy who had combined with him in the preaching of the gospel. He wants to show the Galatians that the controversy is not between one teacher and another, but between truth and error. *Though* has in the Greek text the idea of *even though,* supposing a case which has never occurred. The reference to an angel here could not be, that to the angels also was committed the preaching of the gospel, for Paul knew better than that. It might have reference to the incident referred to in 4:14. The Greek word translated *angel* (*aggelos*) also means a messenger. At Lystra, the Lycaonians witnessed the miraculous healing of the impotent man, and thought that they recognized in Barnabas, the chief of the Greek gods, Zeus. And they thought Paul was Hermes, the messenger and interpreter of the gods (Acts 14:8-18). Paul looks back to the day when the Galatians received him as a messenger of the gods. Thus he says, "But though we or a messenger from heaven." The words *preach gospel,* are from *euaggelizomai,* a verb which means "to announce a message of good news." Paul could have used the Greek verb *kerusso* which means *to announce* and the noun *euaggelion* which means *good news,* but he chose the distinctive verb which in English would be rendered *to evangelize.* The expression *preach gospel unto you,* is literally, *evangelize you.*

Than is from *par' ho,* and the idea is not merely *against* or *besides,* but *beyond,* in the sense of overstepping a limit into a new region. It points out a specific difference. The message of the Judaizers was of an entirely different character. It was intrinsically different. The entire expression in a literal translation would be, *But even though we or a messenger from heaven evangelized you beyond that which we evangelized you.*

Let him be accursed. The word *accursed* is from *anathema.* It is a word used in the LXX,[3] of a person or thing set apart and devoted to destruction, because hateful to God. Hence in a spiritual sense it denotes one who is alienated from God by sin. It cannot refer here to ecclesiastical excommunication, for angels are included. The epistles of Paul attach to the word the idea of spiritual death. Its use in Romans 9:3 where Paul says that he could wish himself accursed from Christ for his brethren's sake, associates it with the further idea of separation from Christ and destruction for all eternity, which is the fate of the unsaved. The word does not, like excommunication, pronounce a judicial sentence on particular convicted offenders, but solemnly affirms general laws of the spiritual kingdom. In I Corinthians 16:22, those who love not the Lord Jesus are declared to be outcasts from the Faith.

Translation. *In fact, even if we or a messenger from heaven preach a gospel to you which goes beyond that which we preached to you, let him be accursed.*

Verse nine. As we said before, so say I now again. The words *said before* are from *prolego* which means "to say beforehand, to predict," and here have the idea of "to say before" in the sense of saying something in times past, since it is used in contrast to the word *now*. The reference is not to verse 8 but to a previous time when Paul made this same statement. The compound verb here and the words *and now,* point necessarily to an earlier time in contrast to the present. It was either said on a previous visit to the Galatian churches or in a letter. The word *now, arti* in the Greek, excludes any reference to the words just

---

3. The Greek translation of the Old Testament, called the Septuagint.

written down. This suggests an already existing danger, and also the fact that Paul had warned the Galatians against the Judaizers even before the latter had made their destructive inroads.

Paul uses the perfect tense here which refers to an act completed in past time having present results. This fact marks this statement not simply as a past fact, but one of which the results remain, doubtless, in that they remember or may be assumed to remember the warning which Paul had given them. This makes the defection of the Galatians all the more inexcusable. The plural number of the verb shows that the previous warning was given not merely by Paul but also by his associates, since the apostle uses the singular verb in the expression, "so say I now again."

If any man preach any other gospel to you, let him be accursed. Paul does not use the Greek conditional particle *ean*, which introduces an unfulfilled condition or an hypothetical case, but he employs *ei* which speaks of a fulfilled condition. It is no longer now a supposition with him, but an assumption of the fact. This conditional particle suggests, not future possibility, but expresses a simple present supposition, and is used often when the condition is known to be actually fulfilled. The result is to bring Paul's statement closer home to the actual case, and applies the anathema directly to the Judaizers. Again, the element of concession or improbability disappears in this statement as it existed in the one preceding, by the omission of the words "we or an angel."

In the words "any other gospel," we have in the original text the idea as before that the "other gospel" was a message that went beyond that preached by Paul, and which therefore passed out of the territory or sphere of Paul's gospel. It was not a perversion of Paul's gospel but a message that was diametrically opposed to it. It was in character, of an opposite nature to Paul's message.

Received is from *paralambano*, a word which means "to appropriate to one's self." It was used of a hospitable welcome such as a host gives to his guest. Such a welcome the Galatians had given the gospel of grace when it was preached among them by the great apostle.

Translation. *Even as we have said on a previous occasion, indeed, now again I am saying, If as is the case, anyone preaches a gospel to you which goes beyond that which ye took so eagerly and hospitably to your hearts, let him be accursed.*

Verse ten. For do I now persuade men or God? Paul feels that the curse which he had just repeated twice over, might strike his readers as unduly harsh and severe. By the use of the word *for,* he introduces an explanatory justification of his stern language. He says that he would not have uttered the statement had he been concerned in influencing men in *his* favor rather than in *God's.* By the use of the word *now,* he argues that at that critical moment when the Galatian Christians were leaning towards the false doctrines of the Judaizers, and a serious and malevolent attack was being made upon the Christian Church and its doctrine of pure grace, it could not possibly be his purpose to curry the favor of men rather than please God. It is as if someone was reproved for undue severity, and he answered, "The severity of my language at least proves that I am no flatterer."

Again, the use of the word *now* could include in it the fact that the Judaizers had caught hold of Paul's statement, "Unto the Jews I became as a Jew, that I might gain the Jews; to them that are under the law, as under the law, that I might gain them that are under the law" (I Cor. 9:20), and had charged him with being a temporizer, a man who changed color with a change in his surroundings in order to ingratiate himself into the good will of men. They charged him with having preached the Mosaic law, because he had become as a Jew to the Jews. He flings out the challenge to the Judaizers to judge *now* whether he was currying the favor of the legalizers. The vehemence of his language was enough to show clearly that he was anything but a turncoat or one who suited his preaching to the whims and the desires of his hearers.

Persuade is from *peitho* which means "to persuade." The more precise meaning in this context is, "to win over, to conciliate and render friendly to one's self." Paul in the use of this word evidently refers to a charge that on previous occasions or in other utterances, he had shaped his words so as to win the favor of men. A similar charge was made by Paul's opponents at Corinth who said that when he was with the Corinthians, he had an abject, servile manner (base), and when he was not with them, he was daring, presumptuous, and over-bold (II Cor. 10:1).

The word *or* is from *e* which means "rather than." This indicates clearly what kind of slanders were being circulated about Paul. His enemies accused him of sacrificing the truth of God for the sake of conciliating men and winning their favor. It was Paul's boast that he became all things to all men, but whereas his real purpose was to win all to Christ, they insinuated that he was more bent on currying the favor of men than securing the approval of God. He had made two concessions to Jewish feeling; he had circumcised Timothy and had recommended for adoption certain regulations tending to promote harmonious intercourse between Jewish and Gentile converts. It was easy to misrepresent these concessions as an abandonment of his former principles.

Or do I seek to please men? These words repeat a little more distinctly the thought of the preceding clause, expressing the idea of attempt more definitely.

Translation. *For, am I at this present moment seeking to win the favor of men rather than the approval of God? Or, am I making it my business to be constantly pleasing men? If I still were pleasing men, in that case, Christ's bondslave I would not be.*

III. *Paul asserts that the gospel he preaches came to him, not from man but directly from God* (1:11-2:21).

  1. *It was a special revelation given to Paul directly from God* (1:11, 12).

Verse eleven. Certify is from *gnorizo*. The word means in general "to make known." But here the Galatians already knew the facts which Paul presents in verses 11 and 12. It has the force here of reminding the Galatians in an emphatic way of what they had already been convinced of. The use of the word *brethren* is a most tender touch on the part of the great apostle. The Greek word is *adelphos*. It means literally, "from the same womb." It means in its purely masculine usage, *a brother*. Here it is plural, and refers to the Galatian Christians as Paul's brethren in Christ. Both Paul and they found the source of their regenerated lives in the work of the Holy Spirit, and thus were children of the same heavenly Father.

Is not after man. Paul's use of the present tense shows the permanence and unchangeableness of his gospel of grace. The distinctive Greek word for *man* here is *anthropos*, the racial term. It speaks here, not of individual men as such, but of the race seen in its human characteristics. The word *after* is from *kata*, the root meaning of which is *down*. The word thus has the idea of domination or control. The specific truth brought out here is that Paul's gospel is not of human origin, is not measured by mere human rules and standards, and is not human in its character.

Translation. *For I make known to you, brethren, the gospel which was announced as good news by me, that it is not as to its nature, human.*

Verse twelve. The word *I* is not here from the person of the verb, but from the word *ego* which is the Greek pronoun meaning *I*. In the Greek language, the verb itself indicates the person doing the acting or representing the state mentioned in the verb, and therefore a pronoun is not needed as in English. That means that when a pronoun is used in connection with a verb, special emphasis is stressed. Paul uses the personal pronoun here to show that he is laying emphasis upon the special education he had received for his ministry of the gospel. He had not, like his converts, learnt it from human teachers, but by direct communion with God, as the Twelve had learnt it from Christ's teaching. Paul is studiously careful to show his independence of the Twelve.

By the use of the pronoun *I*, Paul also compares himself with the Twelve. His thought is, "for neither did I, who, because I was not of the Twelve might be supposed to have received the gospel from man, receive it in that way." The entire tenor of this section indicates that Paul's commission had been declared inferior to that of the Twelve, and that he had this in view when he was defending his apostleship from the attacks of the Judaizers.

The word *received* is from *paralambano* which denotes the act of receiving through communication in general, and directly from the person giving the communication. *Taught* is from *didasko* which refers to the act of receiving, specially through instruction. These were the methods by which the majority of the Christians and even the Christian teachers had received the gospel. Paul says that his was an exceptional case.

The word *revelation*[4] is from *apokalupto* which originally referred primarily to the removal of that which conceals, an uncovering. In some cases the choice of the word seems to be due to the thought of a previous concealment. As it is used in Scripture, it refers to a subjective revelation which either takes place wholly within the mind of the individual receiving it, or is subjective in the sense that it is accompanied by actual perception, and results in knowledge. It has reference to a disclosure to the human mind involving also perception and understanding by the mind. Revelation therefore is the act of God the Holy Spirit uncovering to the Bible writers truth incapable of being discovered by man's unaided reason, this revelation being accompanied by the imparted ability to understand what is uncovered. The time of this revelation of the gospel of grace to Paul was in all probability during his sojourn in Arabia. The words *of Jesus Christ* are in a construction called the subjective genitive. Jesus Christ is the One acting in the noun of action, *revelation*. He did the revealing. He gave the revelation.

Translation. *For, as for myself, neither did I receive it directly from man, nor was I taught it, but I received it through a revelation given me by Jesus Christ.*

>   2. *Paul's previous education could not have been responsible for his teaching of grace, for it was directly opposed to the latter* (1:13, 14).

---
4. *Riches*, pp. 13-21.

Verse thirteen. Paul's argument in this verse is that his early education is a proof that he did not receive the gospel from man. He was brought up in a rigid school of ritualism directly opposed to the liberty of the gospel. He was a staunch adherent of the principles of that school, and as such, relentlessly persecuted the Christian Church. No human agency could therefore have brought about the change. It required the direct interposition of God.

Ye have heard of my conversation. Paul had told the Galatians of his career as a persecutor. It was Paul's habit to include in his preaching the history of his past life as a persecutor (Acts 22 and 26). The word *conversation* is obsolete English for *manner of life,* which latter is the meaning of the Greek word Paul used, *anastrophe.*

The Jews' religion. The word *religion* is not in the Greek text. The Greek word is *Ioudaismos* which refers to the Jewish faith and worship. The term was perhaps coined by the Gentile world as was the name *Christianos,* the name given followers of the Christ (Acts 11:26). The word occurs in II Maccabees where it refers to the Jewish religion as opposed to the Hellenism that the Syrian kings were imposing upon the Jews. As with the case of the name *Christianos*[5] (I Peter 4:14; Acts 26:28), the word *Ioudaismos* conveyed some shadow of the contempt with which the pagan world regarded both Judaism and Christianity. But adopted by the Jews, it would lose the idea of contempt and even become a title of honor, as is the case with the name *Christian*.

Now, the Judaism with which Paul was acquainted and in which his life had been immersed, was apostate. He knew nothing before his conversion, of the supernatural Judaism in which the Levitical sacrifices were the outward expression of an inward faith in a coming substitutionary atonement for sin. Judaism in Paul's time was a mere ethical cult basing salvation on good works, and observing the sacrifices as a mere form. But when he was rethinking the Old Testament economy in the light of

---

5. *Treasures,* pp. 67-70.

the revelations received in Arabia, the supernatural significance of it all opened up to him. But in this verse he is speaking of the apostate Judaism of his early life.

How that beyond measure I persecuted the church of God and wasted it. The words *persecuted* and *wasted* are in the imperfect tense which speaks of continuous action. It describes the course of action continuously pursued by Saul right to the time of his conversion. The word *wasted* is very strong. It referred not merely to an attempt to devastate or ravage, but to ruin and destroy. It applied not only to cities and lands, but also to people. The word was used by the Christians in Damascus, of Saul after his conversion, and it probably became fixed in Paul's mind. The reason why Paul here mentions his attempt to destroy the Christian Church is that he might show that such bitter hostility proved that he was not among those whose association with Christians had led them to receive the gospel.

Paul's use of the term *Church of God* is significant. It shows that Paul at the time of the writing of Galatians, had not only formed the conception of churches as local assemblies, but had already gathered these local churches in his thought into one entity, the universal Church. It also shows that he saw at this time that the nation Israel had been temporarily set aside and the Christian Church brought in, to be the channel through which God was to work for the time being.

Translation. *For you heard of my manner of life aforetime in Judaism, that beyond measure I kept on continuously persecuting the Church of God and continuously bringing destruction upon it.*

Verse fourteen. And profited in the Jews' religion above many my equals in mine own nation. The word *profit* is from *prokopto*, which means "to blaze a way" through a forest, "to cut a pioneer path." Paul means that he outstripped his Jewish contemporaries in distinctively Jewish culture, zeal, and activity. He pioneered in his studies, cutting new paths ahead of his fellow-students. He was a brilliant pupil of Gamaliel.[6] The word *equals* in the

---
6. *Treasures,* pp. 53, 54.

Greek text means, not equals in position but in age. In the words *mine own nation,* we have incidental proof that Paul was writing especially to Gentiles.

Being more exceedingly zealous of the tradition of my fathers. The word *traditions* is from *paradosis* which means literally "to give from the presence of," thus "to give personally." It signifies an act of transmission or that which is transmitted. In the New Testament it is used in the latter sense, without indicating the method of transmission or implying any lapse of time such as is usually associated with the English word *tradition.* The use of the word *fathers* makes it clear that Paul is not referring here to the Mosaic law, but to the instruction received from previous generations. This point is very important. Had Paul lived in his unsaved state in the thought world of the Mosaic economy instead of having his thinking dominated by the Pharisaic traditions, his act of receiving Christ as Saviour would have had some reasonable background, for the Mosaic institutions pointed to a need for Christ and also to the Christ who was needed, the moral law serving the first purpose, the Levitical sacrifices, the second. But Paul is at pains to show his Galatian converts that his salvation and his appointment to the apostleship broke completely with all his background and all his traditions.

He is speaking here of the hereditary traditions of his family. He was the son of a Pharisee. These Pharisaic traditions had been ingrafted on the law and had made that law void (Matt. 15:1-6). Thus, he could not have had a true conception of the Mosaic economy, and when he was converted, he found it necessary to restudy his Old Testament scriptures in the light of the revelations given him in Arabia, and under the instruction of the Holy Spirit. If Paul had intended to refer to the Mosaic law, either by itself or in connection with the Pharisaic traditions, he would have mentioned the law by itself or along with the traditions. He is here speaking of the way in which his brilliant advancement in Judaism had displayed itself. In short, the great apostle before his conversion, was occupied more with human legal enactments and practices as ingrafted upon the Word of God, and as interpreting that Word, than he was with the Word of God itself. The traditions of his fathers included the religious definitions handed down in respect to doctrine, ritual, asceticism, interpretation of Scripture, and conduct of life. Thus, Paul shows that he was not at the time of his conversion and appointment to the office of apostle, under such influences or in such a frame of mind as to make the reception of the gospel by him from human instruction possible. Only a supernatural revelation could have effected it. Therefore, proof is established that neither Paul's office as apostle nor his message came by way of a human channel, but direct from God.

Translation. *And I was constantly blazing a pioneer path, outstripping in Judaism many of my own age in my race, being more exceedingly zealous of my ancestral traditions.*

> 3. Paul could not have learnt the gospel from the Twelve Apostles at Jerusalem, for he kept aloof from them for some time after his conversion (1:15-17).

Verses fifteen and sixteen. But when it pleased God who separated me from my mother's womb. The word *separated* is from *aphorizo* which means "to mark off from a boundary or line." The simple verb *horizo* means "to place a limitation upon, to fix limits around." The cognate noun *horos* means "a boundary, a frontier, a limit." The verb *proorizo* (Eph. 1:5), "to set limits upon beforehand" is there translated *predestinate*. The word *aphorizo* used in our Galatian verse (1:15), is used in Romans 1:1. The impression one gets from the rendering of the A.V. is that it refers to the physical separation of the child from the mother's womb, which idea was not in the apostle's mind. The idea is, "who set me apart, devoted me to a special purpose from before my birth, and before I had any impulses or principles of my own." Passages from the Old Testament sustain this usage (Judges 16:17; Isaiah 44:21, 24, 49:1, 5). This idea is also seen in those instances where a child's destiny is clearly fixed by God before birth as was Samson's (Judges 16:17), and John the Baptist's (Luke 1:15). The preposition *ek* translated *from,* in the phrase "from my mother's womb," is used at times to mark a temporal starting point (John 6:66, 9:1; Acts 9:33, 24:10). Paul, therefore, states that he was set apart or devoted by God to the apostleship before he was born. Here again he shows his apostolic independence of men.

To reveal His Son in me. Does Paul mean here that God called him in order that He might reveal the Lord Jesus *to* Paul, or that He might reveal the Lord Jesus *through* Paul to the world? The answer is found in the meaning and usage of the word translated *reveal, apokalupto*. We will use the terms *subjective revelation* and *objective revelation* in our discussion. A subjective revelation would be one in which God revealed the Lord Jesus to Paul, and an objective revelation, one in which God would reveal Him through Paul to others.

The word *apokalupto* refers to the disclosure of something by the removal of that which hitherto concealed it, and refers especially to a subjective revelation to an individual. A public disclosure of the Lord Jesus through Paul would necessitate the fact that He had been previously hidden from public knowledge, which is not the case, since He had already been preached in the world. But He had been previously hidden from Paul, which points to a subjective revelation of the Lord Jesus to Paul within Paul. Furthermore, if it were an objective revelation through Paul, the Greek would require the preposition *dia* which means *through*. Again, the entire context has to do, not with how Paul *preached* the gospel, but how he *received* it.

Paul makes a distinction between the call and the revelation. The latter cannot then be identified with the previous vision of the Lord Jesus which Paul had on the road to Damascus. That vision was apprehended by the eye. The revelation of which he is speaking here was an inward one, apprehended by the spiritual senses, possibly given Paul during the three days which he spent in communion with his new found Saviour and Lord in Damascus. Thus, Paul, whom God from before his birth had set apart to be a preacher of the gospel to the Gentiles, and whom God had called into salvation and His service, could not have been dependent upon men for his commission or subject to their control.

The word translated *heathen* is from *ethnos* which referred to foreign nations not worshipping the true God, pagans, Gentiles.

Immediately I conferred not with flesh and blood. It was immediately after Paul's experience on the road to Damascus that he went into Arabia. The word *conferred* deserves careful study. It is *prosanatithemi*. It means "to betake one's self to another for the purpose of consulting him." In pagan writers it was used of consulting soothsayers and the like. It was as if Paul said, "I did not consult with anyone in order to learn the opinion of others as to this revelation I received, or to obtain instruction from them, or guidance, or advice." The words "flesh and blood," refer to mankind in general, with the idea of weakness, frailty, and ignorance. Thus Paul asserts that his commission and message came to him directly from God, and that neither was affected in any way by human intervention.

Translation. *But when it was the good pleasure of the One who set me apart before I was born, and called me by His grace, to give me an inward revelation of His Son in order that I might proclaim Him as glad tidings among the Gentiles, immediately I did not put myself in communication with flesh and blood for the purpose of consultation.*

Verse seventeen. Neither went I up to Jerusalem. Went up is from *anerchomai*. It was used especially of visiting Jerusalem which was situated in the highlands of Palestine. *Katerchomai* was used of the descending journey from the city. The religious position of Jerusalem as the seat of the Temple and the mother-city of the Church, and its geographical position on the central heights of Palestine, were the factors that suggested the expressions "going up" and "going down," when a journey was made to that city and then back to one's home.

The word *before* is from *pro* which is evidently used in its temporal sense. Paul is referring here to those who were apostles before him in point of time. The order of the words in the Greek text, *the before me apostles,* shows that Paul recognized the apostleship of the Twelve as essentially the same in character as his apostleship.

But I went into Arabia. Paul does not state his purpose in doing so, but his statement to the effect that after his conversion he did not consult with anybody but went into Arabia, leads one to the clear inference that he wanted to be alone with God. The word *Arabia* is the transliteration (spelling) of a Hebrew word meaning "an arid, thus a sparsely populated place." He needed to be alone with God. He needed time and isolation in order to think. The revelation of the Son of God had blasted away the foundations of the Pharisaic thought structure which he had been building up with such consumate skill and zeal, and it had come tumbling down in ruins about his head. This revelation also furnished him with another foundation upon which to build a new theological structure. But the replacement of the ruined structure with a new one could not be the work of a day or a month. There in Arabia, isolated from all human contact, alone with God, the great apostle restudied his Old Testament scriptures, not now with the Pharisaic traditions vitiating his thinking, but, led by the Holy Spirit, with the central fact of the Cross of the Lord Jesus as the controlling factor in his meditations. Out of all this study emerged the Pauline system of doctrine as we have it presented in *Romans*.

The word *Arabia* was the term applied by Greek writers from Herodotus down, to the whole or various portions of the vast peninsula between the Red Sea on the southwest, the Persian Gulf on the southeast, and the Euphrates River on the northeast. There is nothing to indicate exactly where in this vast territory Paul went. It is not necessary to suppose that Paul went far from Damascus, for the Arabian deserts were within easy reach of that city. It is not likely that Paul went to Mt. Sinai, as some suggest, for that would have constituted too effective an argument for the divine origin of his apostleship, to be omitted here. Furthermore, Sinai was a long way from Damascus, the journey was at all times dangerous for travellers without armed escorts, and in A.D. 37, the most probable year of Paul's conversion, a war between King Aretas and the Romans was in progress, which fact would have made such a journey very doubtful.

GREEK NEW TESTAMENT 53

Translation. *Neither did I go up to Jerusalem to those who were apostles before me, but I went away into Arabia, and again returned to Damascus.*

4. *When he did go up to Jerusalem, he only saw Peter and James, only remained fifteen days, and returned without being recognized by the mass of believers* (1:18-24).

Verse eighteen. The words *after three years* do not merely refer to a lapse of time. They are argumentative. Paul is showing all through this section, his entire independence of the Jerusalem apostles. Therefore, the three years have reference, not to the time after his return from Arabia, but to the period of time after his conversion. The word *see* is from *historeo* which means "to inquire into, to find out, to visit." Paul had been suddenly driven out of Damascus (Acts 9:19-25). He went to Jerusalem to become acquainted with Peter and possibly to seek another sphere of labor. The Authorized Version has the name *Peter* which is the English spelling of the Greek word *petros* meaning "a rock." The Greek text has the word *Kephas* which is the Greek spelling of a Chaldaic word meaning "a rock." He mentions his fifteen day stay to show how brief were his conversations with Peter. The reason his visit was so abruptly terminated was that the Hellenistic Jews were seeking his life (Acts 9:29), and also that the Lord Jesus appeared to him in the Temple and ordered him out of Jerusalem since his ministry would not be received by the Jerusalem Jews (Acts 22:17-18).

Translation. *Then after three years I went up to Jerusalem to become acquainted with Kephas, and remained with him fifteen days.*

Verse nineteen. The construction in the Greek indicates that James was one of the apostles Paul saw. He was not one of the Twelve however, since the brethren of our Lord did not believe on Him at the time of the choosing of the Twelve. The expression "James the Lord's brother" means that he was the son of Joseph and Mary by natural generation. He is the same James mentioned in Mark 6:3; Galatians 2:9, 12; I Corinthians 15:7;

Acts 15:13, 21:18. It is supposed that he was led to believe in the Lord Jesus by reason of the fact that he saw our Lord in His post-resurrection ministry (John 7:5; I Corinthians 9:5, 15:7). He was the Moderator of the church in Jerusalem (Acts 15:13, 21:18).

Translation. *But another of the apostles I did not see except James the brother of our Lord.*

Verse twenty. The words, "Now the things which I write unto you," refer primarily and directly to Paul's statements in verses 18 and 19, to the effect that he went to Jerusalem to become acquainted with Peter, that he saw no others of the apostles except Peter and James, and that he remained in Jerusalem only fifteen days. He considered these facts so important in his demonstration of his apostolic independence that he adds the words, "Behold, before God, I lie not."

The strength of Paul's language is explained by the insidious falsehoods of the Judaizers regarding his supposed dependence upon the Twelve. The logical inference is that they had circulated statements to the effect that Paul had spent much time at Jerusalem with the apostles there. He denies this charge most vehemently.

Translation. *But the things which I am writing to you, behold, before the face of God, I am not lying.*

Verse twenty one. This verse records a period of preaching, as indicated by verse 23. The word *region* is from *klimata*. It denotes the fingers of coastland sloping down from the mountains to the sea in northwestern Syria and eastern Cilicia. The name *Syria* is placed first because Paul's ministry at Antioch preceded that at Tarsus, and because Cilicia was subordinate to Syria in the Roman empire, being only a district of the great province of Syria. Here we have about ten years of Paul's life passed over in silence, between his flight from Jerusalem to Tarsus and his return to the former city for the Apostolic Council. These years were spent around Tarsus and Antioch, in Cyprus and Asia Minor.

GREEK NEW TESTAMENT

Translation. *Then I went into the regions of Syria and Cilicia.*

Verse twenty two. In the construction translated *was unknown,* the emphasis is upon a continuous state, literally "I remained unknown." *By face* could be rendered "with respect to the face," that is, they did not recognize Paul when they saw him. He speaks of the churches of Judaea as distinct from the church at Jerusalem. He left this city so abruptly that the Judaean churches had no opportunity to become acquainted with him. Had he been a disciple of the Twelve, his work would have been in Judaea, but because he was not, that showed that he was an independent missionary, and that he was not operating under the supervision of the Jerusalem church and the Twelve. The phrase *in Christ* distinguishes the Christian churches in Judaea from the unconverted Jewish assemblies.

Translation. *But I remained personally unknown to the churches of Judaea which are in Christ.*

Verse twenty-three. Heard is in the Greek text "they kept constantly hearing," emphasis being, not upon the fact of the hearing, but upon their hearing it constantly. *Only* limits the whole statement. This information regarding the apostle was the only exception to their ignorance of Paul. *Faith* does not refer to the body of truth preached by Paul, but to the faith in Christ which he exhorted his listeners to exercise. It was the principle of the Church's life that the Pharisee Saul was aiming to destroy. His aim was the extermination of the Church and its faith in the Lord Jesus. This he tried to accomplish by the ravaging of the faith of individual Christians. *Destroyed* is from *portheo,* which means "to ravage, to overthrow, to make havoc." It is in the imperfect tense which speaks of continuous action in past time. It is not the fact of having destroyed the faith, that is in view here, for Paul never did that, but the continuous process of ravaging and making havoc of the Church.

Translation. *Indeed, they only kept on hearing, The one who used to persecute us at one time, is now announcing the glad tidings of the faith which at one time he was ravaging.*

Verse twenty-four. And they glorified God in me. The verb presents continuous action, literally, *they kept on glorifying. In* is from *en,* a preposition which sometimes designates that which constitutes the ground or basis of an action. This meaning comes from that use of the word which denotes the sphere within which the action takes place. Paul means that his example was the cause of the Judaean churches glorifying God. They found in Paul an occasion and a reason for glorifying God. *Arthur S. Way* translates: "And so in me they found that for which to glorify God." Paul shows the cordial attitude of the churches of Judaea towards himself, contrasting that attitude with the hatred which the Judaizers displayed in their antagonism against him.

Translation. *And they were continually glorifying God (for that which they found) in me.*

5. *When Paul did go back to Jerusalem after some years, he was most careful to maintain his independence of the apostles there. His fellowship with them was on terms of equality. He was not indebted to them for anything* (2:1-10).

Verse one. Then fourteen years after, I went up again to Jerusalem. Paul has shown up to this point how independent he was of the Twelve during the first fourteen years of his Christian life. Now he proceeds to show how independent he was of the Jerusalem apostles at the time of his visit to that city. He had visited Jerusalem since his journey there to become acquainted with Peter, but he does not mention the fact, for his presence in the city at that time had nothing to do with the questions at issue. He went there with Barnabas to bring alms to the poor saints in that city (Acts 11:30). It was during a period of persecution when James the son of Zebedee and Peter were under the power of Herod, and when the other apostles were probably scattered. In Galatians he is interested only in his visits to that city which involved his relation to the Twelve and to the doctrine he preached.

This visit mentioned in Galatians was ostensibly at the time of the church council spoken of in Acts 15:1-29. We have two records of this council, one by Paul (Gal. 2:1-10), and the other by Luke (Acts 15:1-29). They differ in details, but are in agreement about the important facts. We can expect this when we remember that the two records are independent accounts, and that Paul was drawing certain facts from that which transpired at the council for the purpose of using them in his argument, while Luke, approaching the matter from an historian's viewpoint, is merely recording facts as he finds them.

Both accounts speak of the same issue raised at the council, namely, the right of Paul and Barnabas to dispense with the obligation of circumcision in relation to their Gentile converts. The same apostles take part in the council. The result of the discussion is the same, namely, that circumcision was not to be required of Gentile converts. There is therefore no good reason to think that the two accounts present two different occasions.

The reason why Paul mentions this visit to Jerusalem in such detail, is that his act of referring the matter of circumcision to the Jerusalem church and the Twelve was misrepresented as an act of submission and an acknowledgement of his inferiority to the Jerusalem apostles. The facts of the case were, as Paul brings out, that he had procured the condemnation of the Judaizers who had insisted upon circumcision, had been received by James, Peter, and John in brotherly fellowship, and had been accorded full recognition as the apostle to the Gentiles. Thus, the apostle Paul again demonstrates his entire independence of any human authority.

Took Titus with me. The word *took* is from *sunparalambano*, which means "to take along as a companion." Titus was a Greek, and uncircumcised. Paul probably took him along to make of him a test case on the whole question of Gentile circumcision. This shows the determined spirit with which Paul came to the meeting of the council.

Translation. *Then after the space of fourteen years, again I went up to Jerusalem accompanied by Barnabas, having taken along also Titus.*

Verse two. I went up by revelation. This is not inconsistent with the statement in Acts to the effect that the church at Antioch deputed Paul to go to Jerusalem. *By* is from *kata*. The rendering could be, "I went up in accordance or in conformity with a revelation." That is, the church at Antioch could have commissioned Paul to go to Jerusalem, and in addition to that, the Holy Spirit could have spoken directly to him to the same effect. A like instance is seen in the fact that Peter was requested by the servant of Cornelius to go to the latter's home, and God gave him a vision which prepared him for his mission to that Gentile home. Luke narrates the outward cause. Paul speaks of the inward impression made by the Holy Spirit.

Communicate is from *anatithemi*. The Greek word has the following meanings: "to set forth in words; to impart; to communicate with a view to consultation; to set up a thing for the consideration of others." *Preach* is present tense, indicating that Paul was still preaching grace. The word *privately* indicates that he laid before his Jerusalem hearers, his gospel of grace in one or more separate conferences, separate from the general conferences he may have had at Jerusalem.

To them that were of reputation is from *tois dokousin*. The verb involved is *dokeo* which in its intransitive use means, "to seem, to be accounted, reputed." Thus the phrase could be rendered, "to those who were reputed" men of recognized position such as James, Peter, and John. The idea is "to men of eminence." We have the idea repeated in verses 6 and 9, in the phrases "these who seemed to be somewhat," and "who seemed to be pillars." While the wording in the English of the Authorized Version seems to be somewhat ironical, yet the Greek text gives no hint of that. This would be inconsistent with Paul's assertion of fellowship with these apostles, and with his own humility, and it would have defeated his own purpose by that much, which was to show the Galatians that he was on terms of fellowship with them and was recognized by them in his apostolic authority. The word is a term of honor and conveys no tinge of depreciation.

Lest by any means I should run or had run in vain. Paul uses his favorite metaphor, borrowed from Greek athletics,[7] the stadium foot race, in speaking of his missionary career. The words *I should run* are present subjunctive, the rendering therefore being, "Lest I should be running," referring to his apostolic labors in which he was then engaged. The great apostle expresses therefore a fear of present failure together with a fear that his past labors have been of no avail.

But how are we to understand this fear on the part of the apostle? Paul most certainly does not mean that his past fruitful labors which resulted in the conversion of many sinners and the establishment of churches would be rendered null and void simply because they would not have the approbation of the Jerusalem church. It must be that Paul attached great importance to the estimation in which his preaching would be held by the Jerusalem church and the Twelve, and the reaction of the same upon the Roman world. When we think of the strong prejudices of that church situated in the stronghold of apostate Judaism, this feeling of anxiety lest his work be disowned, is certainly a natural thing. His fear was that those in authority in the Jerusalem church, by insisting on the Mosaic ritual, might thwart his past and present efforts at establishing a Church that would be free from all connections with the Mosaic economy which had been set aside at the Cross. Paul saw that in the existing situation, there was danger that his work would be rendered ineffectual by the opposition of the Jerusalem church; that the disapproval of the Twelve would have such repercussions in the Church that his work would be seriously handicapped. He was always careful lest the Jewish law be forced upon the Gentiles, and lest the unity of the Christian Church be broken by a division of the latter into a Jewish and a Gentile branch.

Translation. *And I went up in accordance with a revelation. And I laid before them for their consideration, the gospel which I am preaching among the Gentiles, but privately to those of recognized eminence, lest by any means I should be running or had run in vain.*

---

7. *Bypaths*, pp. 51-57; *Riches* pp. 32-34.

Verse three. It was a bold move on the part of Paul to bring with him to the Jerusalem council, an uncircumcised Gentile, introducing him as a test case. The dispute over the necessity of Gentile circumcision took place at the Antioch Church, and was successfully resisted there. Then the church in that city determined to send its decision to the Jerusalem church to see whether it would or would not sustain its action (Acts 15:1, 2).

But introduces evidence disproving a previously suggested hypothesis. The statement which follows in verse 3 proves that Paul's fears mentioned in verse 2 had been groundless. The word *Greek* is from *Hellen* which means, *first,* a Greek by nationality, *second,* where opposed to Jews, a Gentile, and *third,* in a wider sense, all nations not Jews who adopted Greek learning and customs. Here it means *Gentile. Being* has a concessive force, literally, "although being" a Greek. *Compelled* denies, not the attempt to compel Titus to be circumcised, but the success of the attempt. The context clearly indicates that strong pressure was brought to bear upon the Jerusalem church to impose circumcision upon Gentile converts, Titus being the individual around whom the controversy was waging. The Jerusalem council sustained the decision of the Antioch church to the effect that circumcision was not to be required of Gentile converts.

Translation. *But not even Titus who was with me, although he was a Gentile, was compelled to be circumcised.*

Verse four. Paul now speaks of the group that insisted upon the circumcision of Titus. He calls them false brethren, brought in unawares. There were three parties in the Jerusalem controversy: Paul and Barnabas who maintained that Gentile converts were not to be circumcised, the false brethren who demanded that they be circumcised, and the Jerusalem apostles who for the sake of expediency were urged by the false brethren to insist that Paul and Barnabas require circumcision of their Gentile converts. The false brethren were the Judaizers who were sneaked into the Jerusalem council, whose purpose it was to bring both Jew and Gentile under the Mosaic law. The expression *brought in unawares* is from *pareisago* which means "to bring in alongside," thus, "secretly or surreptitiously brought in." Strabo uses this word when speaking of the introduction of foreign enemies into a city by a faction within the walls. *Who* is from *hoitines,* speaking not only of identity but emphasizing character or nature. These false brethren were running true to type. They could not come in the front door, but were sneaked in the back way. The presence of the article before *false brethren* in the Greek text, indicates that the Galatian Christians knew who these latter were.

Came in privily is from *pareiserchomai,* "to come in alongside," thus, "to come in secretly." The verb is aorist with a pluperfect sense, speaking of the earlier intrusion of these persons into the Christian churches. This indicates a gradual infiltration of these unsaved Jews who had accepted the Lord Jesus as their Messiah, but who knew nothing of salvation through His precious blood, and who clung to the salvation by-works system of apostate and legalistic Judaism, which system they were desirous of bringing into the Church itself. *To spy out* is from *kataskopeo,* which is used in the LXX of the spying out of a city (II Sam. 10:3). The word means "to spy out with a hostile intent," and likens these Judaizers to spies who are bent on discovering to an enemy the weak points in a military position. The liberty here is the Christian's freedom from the Mosaic law which would have been surrendered in principle if the Gentiles at Antioch had been compelled to be circumcised. The phrase "which we have in Christ," gives the causal ground or basis of the Christian's liberty from the Mosaic economy. *Bring into bondage* is from *katadouloo.* The word means, "to reduce to abject slavery." The future tense tells us that it was not merely an intention on the part of the Judaizers, but an attempt which they thought had assured hopes of success.

Translation. *Now it was because of the false brethren who had been surreptitiously brought in, those of such a character that they sneaked in for the purpose of spying out our liberty which we are having in Christ Jesus, with the expectation of reducing us to abject slavery.*

Verse five. We gave place is from *eiko* which means "to yield." *By subjection* is from *hupotage* which speaks of the act of subjecting. It denotes a voluntary act, not one imposed from without.

That the truth of the gospel might continue with you. This was a grave crisis. The entire status of Gentile Christianity was involved in the case of Titus. The question as to whether Christianity was to be merely a modified form of legalistic Judaism or a system of pure grace, was at stake. Justification by faith was on trial. Circumcision would have set it aside. The word *remain* is from *diameno*. The idea of firm possession is present in this compound verb. *With you* is from *pros humas*. The idea is not that of simple rest. The preposition expresses the relation of an active bearing on life. One could translate *for you,* and paraphrase by the words *with a view to your welfare.*

Translation. *To whom not even for an hour did we yield with reference to the particular voluntary submission (demanded), in order that the truth of the gospel might abide for you.*

Verse six. Not only did Paul successfully maintain his position with regard to the matter of Gentile immunity from the obligation of circumcision at the Jerusalem council, but the persons of eminence in the church there, imposed no restrictions nor commands upon him relative to the matter. The expression *these that seemed to be somewhat,* is from the same Greek word translated *reputation* in verse 2, and refers to the apostolic leaders of the church at Jerusalem. The verb *added* which is attached to this phrase, appears at the end of this verse, Paul indulging in one of his departures from his trend of thought in the intervening words, only to race back to it before he leads his readers too far afield. In the words "whatsoever they were, it maketh no matter with me: God accepteth no man's person:" Paul means no disrespect. He is merely asserting his own independence of them, thus by contrast setting off his apostolic authority in the light of their's.

He says that it made no difference with him what their former position was, referring to their former intercourse with the Lord

GREEK NEW TESTAMENT

Jesus. The *knowing Christ after the flesh* (II Cor. 5:16) gives one no position of preeminence in the Church. Furthermore, he says that God is no respecter of persons, literally, "God does not receive the face of a man." He shows no partiality because of a man's natural ability, his position or possessions in the various departments of human society.

Paul says, "It maketh no matter to me." The word is *diaphero* which means "to matter, it is of importance, it makes a difference." It made no difference to Paul who these men were, what position they were holding, and what advantages they had had, so far as his receiving at their hands an apostolic commission was concerned. He had received his direct from God.

These men of eminence, Paul says, added nothing to him. The word *added* is from *prosanatithemi*. It means "to communicate, to impart." In these words Paul says what he began to say at the beginning of the verse. The Jerusalem apostles imposed on him no burden of doctrine or practice, and imparted to him nothing in addition to what he knew.

Translation. *But to be something from (at the hands of) those who were of repute, whatever they were aforetime, is of no importance to me. God accepts not man's person. For those who were of repute imposed nothing on me.*

Verse seven. But contrariwise. Paul states here that instead of the Jerusalem apostles championing the case of the Judaizers as certain had hoped, they came boldly over to Paul's side after they had heard the issue discussed in private conference. The words *when they saw,* gives the reason for the statement which follows. They imply that what the Jerusalem apostles had learned, had led them to give their endorsement to Paul's message and his stand on the matter of Gentile circumcision. Paul speaks of *the gospel of the circumcision* and the *gospel of the uncircumcision.* His thought is not that there are two different gospels, two different types of messages adjusted to the needs of the Jews and the Gentiles respectively. He means that to him was committed the responsibility of taking the gospel of grace to the Gentiles, and that to Peter was given the commission of taking it to the Jews.

Since this point needs to be guarded in these days, we quote some authorities on the matter. *Lightfoot* says that these phrases denote "a distinction in the sphere in which the gospel was to be preached, not a difference in the type of gospel." *Burton* says that the context demonstrates that Paul regarded the distinction between the gospel entrusted to him and that entrusted to Peter as not one of content but of the persons addressed. *Meyer* says that this passage does not refer to two different gospels but to the same gospel to be given to two different groups of individuals, whose peculiarities demanded of the preacher a special adaptation to his distinctive audience. He says that the passage cannot be worse misunderstood than it has been by *Bauer* who maintained that there was a special gospel to the circumcised which maintained the necessity of circumcision, and a special gospel to the uncircumcised which allowed the matter of circumcision to drop. *Burton* again says that the words *circumcision* and *uncircumcision* are genitives of connection denoting to whom the gospel is to be given. The word *gospel* (*euaggelion*) carries its own content of meaning, namely, "a message of good news."

The word *committed* is from *pepisteumai* which latter is in the perfect tense, implying a permanent commission. This word was also a technical word used in the imperial government of Rome. The imperial secretary used the technical expression *pepisteumai, I have been entrusted,* the qualifying word being added which would designate the matter with which he was entrusted.[8] The apostles were the imperial secretaries of the King of kings, the Lord Jesus, to whom was entrusted the writing and propagation of the New Testament message.

Translation. *But on the contrary, when they saw that I had been entrusted with (the responsibility of preaching) the gospel to the uncircumcised as Peter with (the responsibility of preaching) the gospel to the circumcised.*

---

8. *Bypaths,* pp. 20-32.

Verse eight. This verse is a parenthetical statement. It confirms the contents of the preceding verse, namely that God delegated to Paul the responsibility of giving the gospel to the Gentiles, and to Peter, the responsibility of giving the same message to the Jews. Paul's reasoning is as follows. He recognizes without hesitation Peter's apostleship and its divine source. Then he proves that the recognition of his apostleship given by the Jerusalem apostles was merited, because his experience in preaching the gospel among the Gentiles was equal to and like in character to their efforts among the Jews. He says that God who wrought effectually in Peter's work among the Jews, did the same with reference to his work among the Gentiles. All of which means that both Peter and Paul were recipients of the blessing of God in their work for Him, which is tantamount to saying that He gave recognition to each one as an apostle by divine appointment.

The word *wrought* is from *energeo*. When this verb is applied to the work of the Holy Spirit in the heart of the believer, the preposition *en* (in) is used with it.[9] The fact that this word is not used in connection with the words *Peter* and *me*, tells us that this verse is not describing the work of grace in the hearts of Peter and Paul, but the work of God for them in owning and blessing their preaching with the result that souls were saved in each case. This is in line with the context, for it speaks of God's seal of approval resting upon the work of both Peter and Paul, and thus upon their apostleship.

The words *Peter* and *me* are in the dative case, which case designates the person or thing in whose interest or for whom the action in the verb is performed. God wrought for Peter and for Paul. *To* before *apostleship* is from *eis*, which here has the meaning of "with respect to."

Translation. *For He who worked effectively for Peter with respect to (his) apostolate to the circumcision, also worked effectively for me with respect to the Gentiles.*

Verse nine. And when James, Kephas, and John, who seemed to be pillars, perceived the grace that was given to me. James is

---
9. *Nuggets,* pp. 69, 71.

mentioned first by Paul, and for four possible reasons. *First,* Paul showed his respect to the mother-church at Jerusalem and its highly esteemed leader. *Second,* this James was the brother of our Lord. *Third,* he had presided at the Council. *Fourth,* his well-known strictness as to the observance of the Mosaic law gave special weight to his support of Gentile freedom from the law.

The word *pillars* is from *stulos,* which was used to speak of literal pillars or columns of buildings. But it was also a natural metaphor used in the classics as it is used here. The Church was looked upon as a temple of God, and these men, among others, were looked upon as supporters of the Church, men of distinction and prominence. The word *seemed* is from the same Greek word used in verses 2 and 6, *dokeo.* The word does not cast any doubt nor present a supposition, but means here "to repute." That is, these three men were reputed to be pillars of the Church. They were so thought of by the Jerusalem church.

They gave me and Barnabas the right hands of fellowship. The custom of giving the hand as a pledge of friendship or agreement has been found among both the Hebrews and the Greeks. It was probably derived by the Hebrews from some outside source. The custom appears as early as Homer. It is found in an inscription from Pergamum (98 B.C.), where the people of that city offer to adjust the strife between Sardis and Ephesus and send a mediator to give hands for a treaty. The custom is found among the Persians. Images of right hands clasped were often exchanged in token of friendship. An extract from Tacitus says, "The state of the Lingones had sent, according to an ancient institution, right hands, as gifts to the legions, a signal of good will." On Roman coins there often is seen two hands joined, with various inscriptions speaking of concord and agreement.

The word *fellowship* is from *koinonia.* Its use here is illustrated from secular documents in the clause, "My brother on my father's side with whom I have no partnership."[10] The word

---

10. Moulton and Milligan, *Vocabulary of the Greek Testament.*

koinonia defines the compact recognized and sealed by the right hands of fellowship as a partnership, in this case, a partnership in the preaching of the same gospel. It was a mutual alliance, for Paul and Barnabas grasped the proffered hands of James, Kephas, and John.

The details of the compact are found in the words "that we should go unto the heathen, and they unto the circumcision." The agreement therefore was that Paul and Barnabas should go as apostles to the Gentiles, and the Jerusalem apostles were to go as apostles to the Jews, both groups taking the same gospel. The state of things which existed hitherto remained undisturbed. Two nationally different spheres were to be evangelized with one and the same message. But the agreement was more than this. It was an acknowledgment of apostolic equality. Paul would not be content with the mere approbation of the Twelve upon his missionary labors. He needed to show the Galatians that he was an apostle equal in rank to the apostles at Jerusalem. In addition to that, he deemed it necessary to show them that his contention for Gentile freedom from the obligation of circumcision was sustained in the Jerusalem council. However, this mutual understanding did not forbid Paul to minister to the Jews on occasion or prevent Peter from ministering to the Gentiles should the opportunity arise. Paul began his ministry in each new place by preaching to the Jews. Peter preached to the Gentiles in the house of Cornelius, and ministered at the Gentile church in Syrian Antioch.

Translation. *And having come to perceive the grace which was given to me, James, and Kephas, and John, those who in reputation were looked upon as pillars, gave to me and Barnabas the right hands of fellowship, to the end that we should preach the gospel to the Gentiles and they themselves to the circumcision.*

Verse ten. *Only,* that is, one item in the agreement was emphasized, the care of the poor. This is not a request added to the agreement, but a part of the agreement itself. *Remember* is from *mnemoneuo.* This is the only instance in the New Testament where this word means "to remember" in the sense of "benefit or care for." The force of the tense and mode of the verb causes us to translate, "that we should keep on remembering the poor." Paul and Barnabas had done this before when they brought relief to the poor at Jerusalem on a previous occasion (Acts 11: 27-30). Judaea often suffered from famine, and the Christians there were perhaps the worst sufferers because of the ill-will and persecution which came from the unsaved Jews. This passage implies that there was a state of chronic poverty there, as does Paul's efforts in collecting money on his missionary journeys. He was not attempting to meet an emergency, since it took more than a year to collect the fund, the latter being organized to meet a permanent demand for continuous help.

The word *forward* is from *spoudazo* which means not only "to be willing, to do with eagerness," but "to make diligent effort." It does not refer merely to the apostle's state of mind, but to his activity in relieving the necessities of the poor saints at Jerusalem.

Translation. *Only that we should keep on remembering the poor, which very thing I have made a diligent and eager effort to do.*

6. *But Paul's independence of the Twelve is not only seen in his activities at Jerusalem, but in his act of rebuking Peter at Antioch when the latter was yielding to pressure from the legalizers and was adding law to grace, and in that way denying the fundamental of the gospel* (2:11-21).

Verse eleven. In this verse Paul opens the question *as to whether the Jew himself is still bound by the Mosaic law.* In the Jerusalem council, the question was *as to whether the rite of circumcision should be required of the Gentiles.* The particular Mosaic legislation to which Paul had reference here and which he presented as a test case before the Galatians, had to do with the Levitical legislation regarding the eating of certain foods. While one purpose of the giving of this legislation permitting the eating of certain foods and the prohibition regarding other foods, was a dietary one to promote the physical well-being of the Jews, yet another was that of keeping the Jews a separate people from the Gentiles, thus preserving clean the channel which God was using to bring salvation to the earth. The forbidden foods were found on the tables of the Gentiles. Hence a Jew could never accept a dinner invitation of a Gentile. This was one of the factors which kept the nation Israel apart from the Gentile world.

God had made clear to Peter that this legislation was set aside at the Cross, by the vision He gave him while he was on the housetop of Simon the tanner, with the result that Peter was willing to go to the home of Cornelius (Acts 10). This occurred before the incident to which Paul refers in these verses. When Peter came to Antioch, he saw Jews and Gentiles eating together, and joined their fellowship. When certain Jews from the Jerusalem church came as representatives of James, and saw Peter eating with the Gentiles, they contended that he was going against Levitical legislation. They brought pressure to bear upon Peter, and he discontinued his practice of eating with the Gentiles. This caused the Jews in the church at Antioch to cease eating with the Gentiles, and brought about a division in the church. Paul, in resisting Peter, thus showed that he not only refused to take orders from the Jerusalem apostles, but on the other hand felt that his apostolic position gave him the right to stand openly against them in matters of wrong conduct. In no way could he have better demonstrated his independence as an apostle.

The word *but* introduces the contrast between the fellowship of Paul with the Jerusalem apostles and his attitude against them. The word *withstood* is from *anthistemi* which means "to set one's self against, to withstand, resist, oppose." This verb usually implies that the initial attack came from the other side. It was Peter, in Paul's mind, who was the aggressor. Although not intentional, yet in effect it was an attack on the position which Paul was maintaining at Antioch.

The words, "he was to be blamed," are from *kataginosko* and *eimi*. The literal meaning of the former word is "to know (someone) down," thus "to condemn" someone. The tense of the participle, perfect, and that of the verb, imperfect, gives us "he stood condemned," and that in a continuous fashion. He stood condemned by the Christians of Antioch. The public judgment had turned against him. The intrigue of the Jerusalem Jews at Antioch, the purpose of which was to affix the stigma of uncleanness on the uncircumcised Gentile Christians, was countenanced by Peter and Barnabas. Peter's offensive behavior aroused the indignation of the Antioch Christians. Paul could not therefore keep silence, but was forced to rebuke Peter.

Here the argument for Paul's apostolic independence has come to the highest level yet attained. In Jerusalem Paul faced Peter as an equal in rank and in the gospel ministry. At Antioch he faced him as his superior in character and courage.

Translation. *But when Kephas came to Antioch, to his face I opposed him, because he stood condemned.*

Verse twelve. For before that certain came from James, he did eat with the Gentiles. It is clear that these men were sent by James, men of importance as is shown by the deference with which Peter treated them, and the obsequiousness with which he bowed to their requests. They were not from the ranks of the Judaizers, for James would not send men of that stamp, but Jewish Christians of Jerusalem who like James were still most scrupulous in their obedience to the Mosaic law. James, even after the decision of the council at Jerusalem regarding the relation of the law to Gentile converts to Christianity, still held to the view that the Jewish converts were under the law. James was the occasion of Paul's lapse when the apostle at his request took upon himself a Jewish vow to show the Jews in Jerusalem that he was still a strict Jew (Acts 21:18-26). Here he was the occasion of Peter's lapse when he sent this mission to Antioch with the purpose of enforcing the Mosaic law so far as the Jewish Christians were concerned. News had reached Jerusalem that Jewish and Gentile Christians were eating together, hence the mission from James.

The words *eat with* are from *sunesthio*. The verb is in the imperfect tense. The preposition *sun* prefixed to the verb implies close fellowship or cooperation. The tense of the verb tells us that it was a practice of Peter to eat with the Gentiles. The preposition speaks of the fact that in the act of joining in their meals, not only in the Christian love-feast which was connected with the worship program of the local church, but also in their homes, Peter was on terms of the greatest intimacy. The love-feast was recognized as the bond of fellowship in the infant church.

The probable origin of the Antioch practice of Jew and Gentile eating together, was that the church argued that since the Jerusalem council had upheld the position of Paul on the freedom of the Gentiles from the obligation of circumcision, that all restrictions of the Mosaic economy had been set aside. This would include the Levitical legislation regarding foods. The foods previously forbidden the Jew and found on Gentile tables, now could be included in his menu. Accordingly, the Jewish and Gentile Christians welcomed the opportunity of Christian fellowship at meals. This practice could not have been in force before the Jerusalem council, for, had it been, that question would also have been dealt with. Peter, finding this situation at Antioch, fell in with it in his usual impetuous way. The church at Jerusalem, hearing of his actions, sent this deputation to investigate. These men sent by James, found Peter eating with the Gentiles.

The word *withdrew* is from *hupostello*. This word was used frequently to describe strategic military operations. This suggests that it was part of Peter's strategy in the circumstances with which he was faced. Polybius used this word of the drawing back of troops in order to place them under shelter. This suggests a retreat on the part of Peter from motives of caution. The tense is imperfect, indicating that Peter did not start his withdrawal from the Gentile tables at once, but gradually, under the pressure of their criticism. It gives a graphic picture of the Jerusalem apostle's irresolute and tentative efforts to withdraw from an intercourse that gave offence to these visitors. The verb also was used of furling the sails of a boat. Peter, the former fisherman, was expert at that. Now, he was trimming his sails in a controversy that involved Jewish freedom from the Mosaic law which had been set aside at the Cross.

The word *separated* is from *aphorizo*. It is also in the imperfect tense, speaking of a gradual separation. *Hupostello* describes the partial withdrawal of Peter, and *aphorizo* the complete and final separation from the combined fellowship of the Jewish and Gentile meals, both the common meal eaten at the church, the love-feast, and the meals eaten at the homes of the Gentiles. The whole incident is characteristic of Peter. He was always the first to recognize great truths and the first to draw back from these truths. Witness his great confession of the deity of the Lord Jesus, and so soon after, his repudiation of the prediction of our Lord to the effect that He would soon die at Jerusalem and be raised again (Matt. 16:13-23); also his call to preach (Matt. 4:18-20), and his action of returning to his fishing business instead of fulfilling his commission of preaching the gospel (John 21:3).

Translation. *For before certain from James came, with the Gentiles it was his habit to eat meals. But when they came, he began gradually to draw himself back, and began slowly to effect a final separation, fearing those of the circumcision.*

Verse thirteen. This verse gives the result of Peter's action in the church at Antioch. The Jewish Christians there refused to eat anymore with their Gentile brethren in the Lord. The church was split wide open on the issue. The love-feast, that bond of fellowship expressive of Christian love amongst the brethren, was divided into two groups. The friendly groups of Jews and Gentiles in the fellowship of the homes were discontinued. The fact that the Jews of the Antioch church followed Peter in his withdrawal from the Gentiles, shows that the entire group had eaten with the latter.

Paul says that the Jews *dissembled* with Peter. The word is from *hupokrinomai,* which speaks of the act of concealing one's real character under the guise of conduct implying something different. The word itself means literally "to answer from under," as an actor who speaks from under a mask. Our word *hypocrite* comes from this Greek word. It usually referred to the act of concealing wrong feelings or character under the pretence of better ones.

But in the present case, the knowledge, judgment, and feelings which were concealed, were worse only from the viewpoint of those who had come from Jerusalem of whom Peter and the Antioch Jews were afraid. From Paul's viewpoint, it was their better knowledge which they covered up by their misconduct, the usual type of hypocrisy that proceeds from fear. Paul, by characterizing their actions as hypocrisy, implied that there had been no real change of conviction on the part of Peter and the rest of the Jews, but only conduct that misrepresented their true convictions.

But now regarding Barnabas, and the fact that he was swept off his feet and carried away with their hypocrisy. It was bad enough for Paul, the apostle to the Gentiles and the champion of Gentile liberty from the law, to have Peter act as he did. But the hypocrisy of Barnabas was the cruel blow. With the single exception of Paul, Barnabas had been the most effective minister of the gospel in the conversion of the Gentiles. He had been deputed with Paul by the Antioch church to the council at Jerusalem as its representative. He had come back with the news that the position held by Paul and himself with regard to Gentile freedom from circumcision had been sustained by the Jerusalem apostles. Now, his withdrawal from social fellowship with the Gentiles, came with the force of a betrayal to Paul and the church at Antioch. The defection of Barnabas was of a far more serious nature with regard to Gentile freedom than the vacillation of Peter. Barnabas was Paul's chief colleague in the evangelization of the Gentiles, and now to have him play the hypocrite and deserter, was a bitter blow to the great apostle. This may well have prepared the way for the dissension between them which shortly afterwards led to their separation (Acts 15:39). Barnabas, the foremost champion of Gentile liberty next to Paul, had become a turncoat.

Translation. *And the rest of the Jews also played the hypocrite jointly with him, so that even Barnabas was swept along with their hypocrisy.*

Verse fourteen. The word translated *uprightly* is from *orthopodeo*. *Orthos* means *straight,* and *pous,* which has the same root as the verb *podeo,* means *foot,* literally "to walk with straight feet," thus "to walk a straight course." It speaks of straightforward, unwavering, sincere conduct in contrast to a crooked, wavering, and more or less insincere course such as Paul had said Peter and the other Jews were guilty of. Keeping in mind the foregoing definition of the Greek word we could say, "But when I saw that they walked not orthopedically," that is, in a straightforward, unwavering, and sincere way.

The words *according to* are from *pros,* and put definite limitations upon the words *walked uprightly*. The sense here is not that Peter failed to walk in conformity to the precepts of evangelical truth, but that his attitude towards the truth of the gospel was not straightforward. The idea is, "He did not pursue a straight course in relation to the truth of the gospel." He did not deal honestly and consistently with it. His was an attitude that led him to juggle with its sacred truth, to warp it, to misrepresent it, to deal crookedly with it. What an indictment of Peter.

Before all is from *emprosthen panton*. Paul's rebuke of Peter was in the sight of the whole Antioch church, in the presence of everybody. The fact that the article is absent before the word *all* makes it a general statement. The rebuke was not given before the officers of the church only, or before a specially convened and restricted number of people, but right in open church meeting and before all the members of the Antioch church who were present. *Augustine* said, "It is not advantageous to correct in secret an error which injured openly."

If thou being a Jew, livest after the manner of the Gentiles, and not as do the Jews, why compellest thou the Gentiles to live as do the Jews? The word *live* here, from *zao,* does not refer to the moral living according to Gentile or Jewish fashion, but to the shaping of the life with reference to the external social observances in the Christian fellowship, such as Levitical restrictions on eating. The present tense of *live* must not be pressed to the point of teaching that Peter at the time of this rebuke, was living as the Gentiles do, for he was not. It describes a mental attitude or habit which had in times past shown itself in outward actions, and which was still in force, but which was being hypocritically covered up by Peter's action of withdrawing from fellowship with the Gentiles. It shows that Peter had not in principle abandoned it, but had trimmed his sails to the sudden change of wind that came from Jerusalem. Paul, in his rebuke, forcibly sets forth Peter's inconsistency in compelling the Gentiles to obey the Levitical legislation regarding foods, for the Gentiles had only one of two choices in the premises, either to refuse to obey the law in this respect and thus cause a split in the Christian Church, or to preserve harmony by coming under the law. And the apostle Peter did all this with a full understanding of the vision God had given him, which clearly taught him that the Levitical legislation for the Jew was now a thing of the past (Acts 10:28), and that the line of separation had been broken down between Jew and Gentile by the Cross.

Peter's action of refusing to eat with the Gentiles, did not merely have the effect of maintaining the validity of the law for Jewish Christians, but it involved the forcing of that law upon the Gentile Christians, that, or creating a wide-open division in the Church. This latter was what concerned the apostle Paul. He deemed it of utmost importance to maintain the unity of the Christian Church as against any division into Jewish and Gentile groups. At the Jerusalem council he had agreed to a territorial division of the missionary field into Gentile and Jewish divisions, but to create a division between Jew and Gentile in a Gentile community and church, was out of the question and was something not to be permitted.

At the Jerusalem council, it was agreed that the Jewish Christians should continue to keep the law, and that the Gentile Christians were to be free from the law. But this arrangement left the question undecided as to which decision of the council should take precedence when an issue arose such as we see at

Antioch where Peter's action brought pressure to bear upon the Gentiles. Paul insisted that in such an instance, the Jews were not obligated to keep the law.

Translation. *But when I saw that they were not pursuing a straightforward course in relation to the truth of the gospel, I said to Kephas in the presence of everybody, If you, being a Jew, habitually are living after the manner of the Gentiles, and not after that of the Jews, how is it that you are compelling the Gentiles to live after the Jewish manner?*

Verse fifteen. The word *we* is emphatic and serves to emphasize the sharp contrast which Paul is about to make between the Jew and the Gentile. The Greek verb carries its own person in itself, and when the pronoun is used with it, the writer wishes to call particular attention to the subject of the verb. The translation could thus read, *As for us, by nature we are Jews, not sinners of the Gentiles.* The word *sinners* is not here used in its strict sense where it speaks of persons guilty of sin and thus not righteous, but as it is often used in the New Testament, of persons from the point of view of the speaker or from that point of view which he was momentarily holding, who were preeminently sinful, sinners above others, or habitual sinners. The phrase "publicans and sinners" is an example. It was the Pharisaic point of view in relation to persons guilty of specific violations of the law. The Jews so regarded the Gentiles whom they spoke of as unclean and dogs. Paul is here speaking to Peter on the common ground of their former Judaism and in an ironical fashion using the language of Judaism.

In the word *we,* Paul includes himself, Peter, and the Jewish Christians at Antioch in contrast to the Gentile Christians. He says that he and they are Jews by birth, not only not Gentiles, but not even Gentile proselytes. He implies that as such, the Jews have special privileges and prerogatives.

Authorities differ on the question as to whether verses 15-21 are part of Paul's words to Peter in the hearing of the Antioch church, or whether Paul's words in verse 14 are all that is reported of what he said to him on that occasion, and that verses

15-21 are specially written to the Galatians as an answer to the question of Paul. The matter is not important, but the writer leans toward the opinion that they are part of what Paul said to Peter, and for the following reasons. The bare reproach of verse 14 would hardly be in keeping with the serious nature of the trouble at Antioch. Again, it would be too brief an extract from Paul's words to Peter, to show the Galatians that Paul had really come to grips with Peter on the question at issue. In the third place, Paul in 4:1 resumes his direct words to the Galatians in the expression "O foolish Galatians."

Translation. *As for us, we are Jews by nature, and not sinners of Gentile origin.*

Verse sixteen. The word *law* here is used in its qualitative and legalistic sense. It denotes divine law looked upon as a purely legalistic system. It consists of statutes. If a person obeys the law, he secures thereby the divine approval. If he disobeys it, he is subject to divine condemnation. The divine approval is a matter of debt which God owes and pays to the person who obeys. This is a salvation which the person merits, and which is given on the basis of works, not grace. We must be careful to note that the Bible nowhere teaches this concept of divine law so far as a lost sinner is concerned, and with reference to his salvation from sin. This concept had its origin in the thought and practice of man all down the ages since its inception in the heart of Cain. Paul had held this view as a self-righteous Pharisee. The commandment which he thought was ordained to give life, he found to be a ministration of death (Rom. 7:10). He admits, that with all the racial superiority and privileges inferred in what he says in verse 15, that even Jews found out that they could not be declared righteous by virtue of their obedience to the legal enactments of the Mosaic law.

But is not adversative but exceptive. *Faith* here refers to the acceptance of that which accredits itself as true, and a corresponding trust in the person concerning whom the facts are presented. The expression, *of Jesus Christ,* is an objective genitive, corresponding to another construction in Greek which is translated *in*

Jesus Christ. *By* is from *dia* which means *through,* and it indicates the channel through which one secures salvation.

The word *justified* is from *dikaioo.* The cognate noun is *dikaiosune* which means *righteousness.* Thus the act of God in justifying a believing sinner consists of taking away his guilt and its penalty, since Christ bore both on the cross, and the imputation of a righteousness, even Christ Jesus Himself, in whom the believer stands not only guiltless and uncondemned for time and eternity, but also positively righteous in the sight of the eternal laws of God.

Translation. *And knowing that a man is not justified by law works but only through faith in Christ Jesus, we also placed our trust in Christ Jesus, in order that we might be justified by faith in Christ and not by law works, because by law works there shall no flesh be justified.*

Verse seventeen. The word *if* is from *ei,* referring to a fulfilled condition. The Christian Jews, in seeking to be justified in Christ, were shown to be sinners just like and in the same class as the Gentiles. When they sought justification in Christ and thus by grace, it was an admission on their part that there is no justification by works, that the seeker is not justified, and is therefore a sinner. The attempt to be justified in Christ awakens the consciousness of sin, and compels the Jew to put himself on the plane of the Gentile. The Jew who calls the Gentile a sinner, in seeking to be justified by faith, is forced to admit that he is a sinner also. He has found that the law has failed him as a justifying agency.

Paul repudiates the false assumption of the Judaizers who charged that Christ is the promoter and encourager of sin in that He causes the Jew to abandon the law as a justifying agency, and in doing so, puts himself on the common plane of a Gentile whom he calls a sinner and a dog. The Judaizers argued that in view of the fact that violation of the law is sin, therefore, abandonment of the law in an effort to be justified in Christ is also sin. Thus Christ is the promoter of sin.

The word *by* is from *en* which is used with the instrumental case at times, and means "by means of." But here it is better to use it with the locative of sphere and translate *in Christ,* since Christ is the sphere within which his justification was procured and applied, Christ being his righteousness.

Translation. *But if, as is the case, while seeking to be justified in Christ, we (Jews) ourselves also were found to be sinners, is Christ therefore a promoter of sin? Away with the thought.*

Verse eighteen. In this verse, Paul sustains his statement "Away with the thought." *Build* is from *oikodomeo* which in connection with the law means "to render or declare valid." *Destroy* is from *kataluo* which applied to the law means "to deprive of force, to abrogate." Paul is really referring to Peter's action of declaring the Levitical legislation regarding the eating of food, null and void by his eating with the Gentiles, and then declaring it valid by his act of withdrawing from that fellowship. But he tactfully puts himself into the picture and supposes an hypothetical case. His argument is to the effect that instead of committing sin by abandoning the law for grace, one becomes a transgressor by returning to the law which he has abandoned.

The word *transgressor* is from *parabates*. This word seems to have been chosen by the inspired apostle rather than the term used so far in the discussion, namely, *sinner,* from *hamartolos,* to get rid of the ambiguity of the latter word as it was used in this context. *Parabates* refers to one who disregards the ethical spirit of the law, *hamartolos,* to one who disregards the letter of the law. The use of the former word rather than of the latter, emphasizes the point here that one who is obedient to the statutes of the law yet may miss the real meaning of the law. Peter, by withdrawing from fellowship with the Gentiles, was obeying the letter of a law he knew had been set aside by God, and was ignoring its significance, namely, that of a temporary measure for the time of the Old Testament dispensation, to be abrogated at the Cross. Peter became a transgressor in that he, declaring by his conduct that the law was null and void, now declares valid again that which he destroyed, thus admitting his guilt in that destruction. The word *make* is from *sunistemi* which means here "to exhibit in one's conduct."

Translation. *For if the things I tear down, these again I build up, I exhibit myself as a transgressor.*

Verse nineteen. Paul's use of the word *law* in this verse must be governed by its use in the context. The words, "works of the law" of verse 16, speak of the divine law conceived of as a means of acceptance with God in the case of the sinner who obeys it. Paul does not say that he is dead to law, that is, a law to himself, thus a lawless individual. He still holds to the great ethical principles of love and justice, for instance, which are eternal in their significance, the great underlying principles that inhere in God's character and in His government. When Paul says that he has died to a thing he means that he has ceased to have any relation to it, so that it has no further claim upon or control over him. It is law as conceived of as a body of legalistic statutes, that he has died to. He uses the personal pronoun *ego,* which indicates that he is speaking of his own personal experience. His attempt to fulfil the requirements of the Mosaic legislation as a means of salvation, had taught him his own inability to meet its demands, and its inability to make him righteous. Thus he finally abandoned it as a means of justification, and accepted salvation in Christ. He found that what the law did was to reveal sin, to provoke sin, in a certain sense, to create sin, for where there was no law, sin was not reckoned. He found that it provided no remedy for sin, but rather condemned him hopelessly, for no one can fulfil its requirements. It exercised a double power over him, for it made him a sinner and punished him for being one. The poet says, "Do this and live, the law commands, but gives me neither feet nor hands. A better word the gospel brings. It bids me fly and gives me wings."

Faith in Christ was the means whereby Paul's complete and irreparable break with the law was effected. The Lord Jesus

lived under the law, fully obeyed that law, assumed th[e]
and penalty which the human race incurred by having vi[olated]
the law, and in dying under the law satisfied its requirements.
Thus he passed out of the realm where law in its legalistic
aspect had control over Him. All believers were identified with
Christ in His death and also in His resurrection, and thus have
passed out of the realm of divine law so far as its legalistic aspect
is concerned.

He says that he has thus died to the law that he might live
unto God. Subjection to the law as a means of acceptance with
God, in reality prevented him from living a life of unreserved
devotion to God. This is one of the most grievous vices of
legalism, that it comes between the soul and God.

Translation. *For, as for myself, I through the intermediate
agency of the law died to the law, in order that I might live
with respect to God.*

Verse twenty. I am crucified with Christ. The verb is in the
perfect tense which speaks of a past completed action having
present finished results. Paul uses it to show that his identification with Christ at the Cross was a past fact, and that the
spiritual benefits that have come to him through his identification
are present realities with him. By this statement he also shows
how he died to the law, namely by dying with Christ who died
under its penalty. The law's demands were satisfied and therefore have no more hold on Paul. But thus being crucified with
Christ, meant also to Paul, death to self. When Paul died with
Christ, it was the Pharisee Saul who died. What he was and
did up to that time passed away so far as he was concerned.
Saul was buried, and the old life with him. The dominating
control of the Adamic nature had its power over him broken.

Nevertheless I live. Saul the self-righteous Pharisee, died, but
Paul the great apostle, lives. The *ego* remained.

Yet not I, but Christ liveth in me. It is no longer a self-cen-
tered life that he lives, but a Christ-centered one. His new life
is a Person, the Lord Jesus living in Paul. And through the
ministry of the Holy Spirit, the Lord Jesus is manifest in his

life. The new life is no longer, like the former one, dependent upon the ineffectual efforts of a man attempting to draw near to God in his own righteousness. The new life is a Person within a person, living out His life in that person. Instead of attempting to live his life in obedience to a set of rules in the form of the legal enactments of the Mosaic law, Paul now yields to the indwelling Holy Spirit and cooperates with Him in the production of a life pleasing to God, energized by the divine life resident in him through the regenerating work of the Spirit. Instead of a sinner with a totally depraved nature attempting to find acceptance with God by attempted obedience to a set of outward laws, it is now the saint living his life on a new principle, that of the indwelling Holy Spirit manifesting forth the Lord Jesus. That is what Paul means when he says: *And the life which I now live in the flesh, I live by the faith of the Son of God, who loved me and gave Himself for me.*[11]

Translation. *With Christ I have been crucified, and it is no longer I who live, but there lives in me Christ. And that life which now I live in the sphere of the flesh, by faith I live it, which faith is in the Son of God who loved me and gave Himself on my behalf.*

Verse twenty one. Frustrate is from *atheteo* which means "to do away with something laid down, presented, or established, to act towards anything as though it were annulled, to thwart the efficacy of anything, to nullify, to make void." All these meanings could be applied here to the act of adding law-works to faith as the ground of a sinner's justification. One may preach that Christ died for our sins, but if he adds works to faith as the means of the acceptance of the salvation Christ procured for lost sinners at the Cross, he has thwarted the efficacy of grace, for the fundamental meaning of grace is that salvation is given free, without money and without price. *There is no salvation for the sinner who depends in the least upon good works as a means of acceptance with God.*

If righteousness is imputed on the basis of obedience to law, then, Paul says, Christ is dead in vain. The words *in vain*

---
11. *Riches*, pp. 74-78, 103-114.

are from *dorean* which means literally, *without a cause.* That is, if a person could be saved by keeping the law, then there would be no need for the death of Christ. He would have died without a cause, needlessly.

Translation. *I do not thwart the efficacy of the grace of God. For if through law comes righteousness, then Christ died without a cause.*

DOCTRINAL

Paul defends his doctrine of justification by faith alone without works, against that of the Judaizers who taught that the works of an individual gave him acceptance with God (Ch. 3 and 4).

I. *The Galatian Christians received the Holy Spirit in answer to their faith in Christ, not through obedience to law* (3:1-5).

Verse one. Paul says, *O foolish Galatians.* It is an expression of surprise mingled with indignation. The situation in Galatia will help us understand this outcry. There was on the one hand, the native and national spirit joined to the power of the priesthood and the temples, the spirit of Orientalism, that of stagnation, ignorance, and superstition. On the other hand, there was the desire for education, the recognition that Greece and Rome stood on a higher intellectual level than was afforded by the native religions and customs, and in addition to that, a revolt against the ignorant and enslaving native superstitions. The people of the province of Galatia are those who have shaken off the benumbing and degrading influence of the native magic and superstition. They are those who judge for themselves as to the real values in life, and lay claim to insight and wisdom. Paul accuses them with failing to use that insight and wisdom, that appreciation of the better things, when he uses the Greek word translated *foolish.* The word is *anoetos.* It denotes the stupidity that arises from deadness and impotence of intellect. It means "lacking in the power of perception, unwise." It refers to one who does not reflect. The word speaks of failure to use one's powers of perception. The Galatians, Paul says, were certainly not using their heads. The word is used with an ethical reference as the faculty of moral judgment. Thus the word indicates a failure to use one's powers of perception, that failure being due to a moral defect. It is always true, as it was with the Galatians, that the act of a Christian who embraces false doctrine, is due to sin in his life. The Galatian defection was not due to any fickleness of the Gauls. They are not prominent in the picture. Paul sends this stinging rebuke therefore, "*O Galatians, who fail in the first characteristic of the Galatians, namely, the ability to use their heads and to appreciate the finer values of life.*"

Who hath bewitched you? The word *bewitched* is from *baskaino*. Paul's metaphor is derived from the popular superstition of the evil eye. The word denoted either the fascination of an evil eye or some malignant influence akin to it. The infatuation of the Galatians is attributed to the baneful effect of some mysterious power of evil.

Before whose eyes Jesus Christ hath been evidently set forth, crucified among you. The words *set forth* are from *prographo*. It is the usual word speaking of the act of posting up public announcements or notices. The word is found in early secular documents where a father posted a proclamation that he would no longer be responsible for his son's debts. It does not here speak of the act of painting the crucified Christ on a placard for public notice, but of posting a public announcement to the effect that He was crucified. This Paul did in his preaching among the Galatians. This placarded notice of the crucifixion of the Lord Jesus should have been enough to keep the eyes of the Galatians from wandering to the enticements of the Judaizers. The word *crucified* is in the perfect tense. This speaks of the fact that the apostle is not speaking of the figure of a dead Christ on a crucifix, but of the risen, ascended Christ who had been crucified, who was alive, whose glorified body still bore the marks of the nails and the scars of the crown of thorns, and who is the living Saviour by virtue of His atoning work on the Cross.

Translation. *O, unreflecting Galatians, who bewitched you,[12] before whose eyes Jesus Christ was placarded publicly as the Crucified One?*

Verse two. We have here a forcible appeal to the experience of the Galatians. By the use of the word *now*, Paul indicates that an answer to the question about to be asked, would be a decisive argument. It is as if Paul said, "I will convince you of your error by this one argument." By the receiving of the Spirit, Paul means the initial entrance of the Holy Spirit into their hearts when they put their trust in the Lord Jesus.

The words "by the hearing of faith," are from *ex akoes pisteos*. The word *akoes* translated *hearing* refers either to the act of hearing a message, or to the message that is heard. The second meaning agrees more with the context since Paul is contrasting his message of grace with the preachments of the Judaizers. The phrase *of faith* defines or describes the message. It is a message that announces faith as the means whereby one receives salvation. The only answer the Galatians could give to this question was that they received the Spirit, not by obedience to the law, but through their faith in Paul's message of grace.

Translation. *This only am I desiring to learn from you. By means of law works did you receive the Spirit or by means of the message which proclaims faith?*

Verse three. In verse 2, Paul speaks of the initial entrance of the Holy Spirit into the hearts of the Galatian Christians when they put their trust in the Lord Jesus. In this verse, he is speaking of the sanctifying work of the Spirit in the lives of these saints. He asks the question, "Are you to such a degree irrational? Having begun your Christian life in dependence upon the indwelling Spirit, are you now being brought on to the state of spiritual maturity by means of self effort?"

The words *made perfect* are from *epiteleo* which means "to bring something to the place where it is complete." The cog-

---
12. The words "that ye should not obey the truth" are a rejected reading.

nate noun is the word Paul uses when he speaks of a spiritually mature Christian, one who is living a well-rounded, well-balanced, mature life.[13] By the word *flesh* here he refers to all that a person is as the product of natural generation apart from the morally transforming power of the Holy Spirit in regeneration. The word speaks of the unsaved man, body, soul, and spirit, controlled by his totally depraved nature, together with all his human accomplishments, positions, capabilities, and philosophies. See the following scriptures as illustrations of this use: John 3:6; Philippians 3:3, 4; Romans 6:19, 7:5, 18, 25, 8:3; II Corinthians 1:17.

The Judaizers in preaching a message of law obedience to the Galatian Christians, caused these latter to abandon the position of grace and put themselves in the sphere of law, both that of the Judaizers' system of legalism, and that of the Old Testament economy. Because there was no provision in the Mosaic economy for an indwelling Spirit who would sanctify the believer as that believer trusted Him for that work, the Galatians were turning away from the teaching and the reality of the ministry of the Spirit in the life of the believer in this dispensation of grace, and were starting to depend upon self effort in an attempt to obey an outward legalistic system of works. Thus these Christians who had begun their Christian lives in dependence upon the Holy Spirit, now were depending upon self effort to continue in them the work of sanctification which the Holy Spirit had begun. The present tense of the verb here indicates that the Galatians had already begun this attempt. Paul says in effect, "How foolish to think that you can bring yourselves to a state of spiritual maturity in your Christian lives. That is the work of the Spirit. Only He can do that for you."

Translation. *Are you so unreflecting? Having begun by means of the Spirit, now are you being brought to maturity by the flesh?*

Verse four. This verse speaks of the sufferings which the Galatian saints went through as a result of having received the

---

13. *Treasures*, pp. 113-121.

Lord Jesus as Saviour. The only record of any persecutions in the Galatian cities is in Acts 14:2, 5, 19, 22. We are left somewhat in the dark regarding these sufferings, their nature and extent. Paul appeals to the Galatians not to let these sufferings be in vain by turning their backs on grace and putting themselves under the legalistic system of the Judaizers. The construction in the Greek text gives the idea, "If it really be in vain." It leaves a loophole for doubt in the apostle's mind that the Galatians really were swinging away from grace to law. It implies an unwillingness on his part to believe this.

Translation. *So many things did you suffer in vain? If indeed they really were in vain?*

Verse five. The word *therefore* continues the thought of verses 2 and 3 which is further emphasized. In verse 2, Paul is speaking of the initial entrance of the Spirit into the hearts of the Galatians at the moment they placed their faith in the Lord Jesus. In verse 3, he refers to the sanctifying work of the Spirit in the believer's life. In this verse, the subject of the *charismatic* manifestations of the Spirit is introduced, namely, the act of the Holy Spirit in enduing certain members of the Galation churches with special gifts of the Spirit. All these Paul brings to bear upon his contention that the *grace* way of salvation must be God's way since it is accompanied by the supernatural ministry of the Holy Spirit.

The construction in the Greek requires us to understand that the One who ministered the Spirit to the Galatians is the same Person who worked miracles among them, namely, God the Father. The word *ministereth* is from *epichoregeo* which means "to supply abundantly or bountifully." The word *miracles* is from *dunamis,* used in I Corinthians 12:10 (miracles), and in II Corinthians 12:12 (wonders). In each place, the reference is to the Holy Spirit conferring miracle-working power upon certain members of the early Church. In the view of Paul, it was the same Spirit who was performing His work of sanctification in the lives of the Galatian saints, who was also bestowing miraculous powers upon them. The present tense of the participles here informs us that the work of the Holy Spirit in both respects was continually going on in the Galatian churches, even at the time of the inroad of the Judaizers, although His work was being hindered by the act of the Galatians slowly turning away from His ministrations and depending instead upon self effort. The point however is that these Galatians still had the attesting power of the miracles among them, proving that grace and not works was the way of salvation. Yet in spite of all this irrefutable proof, they were forsaking the place of grace to take their stand under law. Over against all this, the Judaizers had nothing as an evidence that their message was from God.

Translation. *Therefore, the One who is constantly supplying the Spirit to you in bountiful measure, and constantly working miracles among you, by means of law works is He doing these things, or by means of the message which proclaims faith?*

II. *Abraham was justified by faith, not works. Therefore the true children of Abraham are justified in the same way* (3:6-9).

Verse six. In this section entitled DOCTRINAL (chapters 3 and 4), Paul demonstrates that salvation is by grace and in answer to faith, and not by works. His first proof was based upon the fact that the supernatural ministry of the Spirit which accompanied the act of faith on the part of the Galatians, is a proof that his message of grace was of divine origin, and that the message of the Judaizers which in character was diametrically opposed to it, was of human origin. Now, in these verses, he adduces proof from the fact that Abraham was saved by faith and not by works.

The occasion for his argument is found in the fact that the Judaizers taught that the natural descendants of Abraham were his children, and thus accepted with God. All of which meant that only the circumcised could be saved. Thus, circumcision was a prerequisite of salvation. This teaching was based on a misapprehension of Genesis 12 and 17. They argued that no one could participate in the blessings of God's covenant with Abraham, and so in the Messianic salvation which was inseparably connected with it, unless he was circumcised. The mistake

GREEK NEW TESTAMENT

they made was in failing to distinguish between the purely Jewish and national covenant God made with Abraham, which had to do with the earthly ministry and destiny of the Chosen People as a channel which God would use in bringing salvation to the earth, and that salvation which came through a descendant of Abraham, the Messiah. Circumcision was God's mark of separation upon the Jew, isolating him in the midst of the Gentile nations, in order that He might use the nation Israel for His own purposes. It had nothing to do with the acceptance of salvation by the Jew. Over against this contention, Paul argues that Abraham was justified by faith, not by circumcision. In Romans 4:9, 10, he proves his case conclusively when he shows that Abraham was declared righteous before he was circumcised, which demonstrates that his circumcision had nothing to do with his acceptance of salvation.

We now look at the words, *Abraham believed God, and it was accounted to him for righteousness.*

The word *accounted* is from *logizomai*. It deserves careful study. The word is used in the papyri as a business term: for instance, "*put to one's account;* let my revenues be *placed on deposit* at the storehouse; *reckoning* the wine to him at 16 drachmae the monochore; a single artabae *being reckoned* at 180 myriads of denari; I now give orders generally with regard to all payments actually made or *credited* to the government."[14]

Thus Abraham believed God, and his act of faith was *placed to his account* in value as righteousness. He believed God and his act of faith *was credited to him* for righteousness. He believed God and his act of faith was *placed on deposit for him and evaluated* as righteousness. He believed God and his act of faith was *computed as to its value, and there was placed to his account*, righteousness. He believed God, and his act of faith *was credited to his account* for righteousness. Finally, he believed God, and his act of faith *was credited to him*, resulting in righteousness.

All this does not mean, however, that Abraham's act of faith was looked upon as a meritorious action deserving of reward.

---
14. Moulton and Milligan, *Vocabulary of the Greek Testament.*

It was not viewed as a good work by God and rewarded by the bestowal of righteousness. That would be salvation by works. But the fact that Abraham cast off all dependence upon good works as a means of finding acceptance with God, and accepted God's way of bestowing salvation, was answered by God in giving him that salvation. *Abraham simply put himself in the place where a righteous God could offer him salvation upon the basis of justice satisfied, and in pure grace. God therefore put righteousness to his account. He evaluated Abraham's act of faith as that which made it possible for Him to give him salvation.*

We now come to a study of the Greek word translated *righteousness, dikaiosune,* and the adjective *dikaios,* both having the same root. *Cremer* in his monumental work, *Biblico-Theological Lexicon of New Testament Greek,* has the following to say on these important words: He says that *dikaios* is "what is right, conformable to right, answering to the claims of usage, custom, or right. . . . The fundamental idea is that of a state or condition conformable to order, apart from the consideration whether usage or custom or other factors determine the order or direction. Thus, *dikaios* is synonymous with *agathos* (good), only that *dikaios* is a conception of a relation and presupposes a norm, whereas the subject of *agathos* is its own norm.

"As to the import of the conception in a moral sense, there is a decisive difference not to be mistaken between the profane and especially the Greek usage, and the Biblical, and this difference arises, from the different, nay, opposite standards by which it is estimated in the two spheres. *Righteousness in the biblical sense is a condition of rightness the standard of which is God, which is estimated according to the divine standard, which shows itself in behavior conformable to God, and has to do above all things with its relation to God, and with the walk before Him. It is, and it is called dikaiosune theou (righteousness of God) (Rom. 3:21, 1:17), righteousness as it belongs to God, and is of value before Him, Godlike righteousness, see Ephesians 4:24; with this righteousness thus defined, the gospel (Rom. 1:17) comes into the world of nations which had been wont to measure by a different standard. Righteousness in the Scripture sense is a thoroughly religious conception, designating the normal relation of men and their acts, etc., to God. Righteousness in the profane mind is a preponderatingly social virtue, only with a certain religious background. . . . In pagan Greece the dikaios (righteous) person is he who does not selfishly nor yet self-for-gettingly transgress the bounds fixed for him, and gives to everyone his own, yet still desires what is his, and does not in the least withdraw the assertion of his own claims, a view which Christianity has continually to combat.*[15, 16]

"In its scriptural sense, both in the Old Testament and New Testament, righteousness is the state commanded by God, and standing the test of His judgment (compare II Cor. 3:9), the character and acts of a man approved of Him, in virtue of which the man corresponds with Him and His will as his ideal and standard, compare Ephesians 4:24; or more generally it denotes the sum-total of all that God commands, of all that He appoints. As God Himself is thus the standard of this righteousness, it is *dikaiosune theou,* a righteousness as it belongs to God or to itself for God, is well pleasing to Him, Godlike righteousness. . . . Just such a righteousness that ought to be the goal of human effort and desire, St. Paul insists upon as, strictly speaking, the Scripture conception of *dikaiosune* (righteousness), and as the result of the New Testament salvation realized or to be realized in man."

This righteousness Cremer describes as "a state of the subject who stands God's judgment, who having fulfilled all obligations, has no guilt to hide. . . . The righteousness of God is a state called forth by God's act of justification, namely, by judicial disengagement or release from all that stands in the way of being righteous, a liberation of which man becomes a partaker by means of faith. . . . We see therefore that the Pauline conception of righteousness — which as to form always expresses a relation to the judgment of God — includes this special feature,

---

15. Italics ours.
16. See Paul's classical use of this word in Romans 5:7; also of *agathos* (good).

namely, it denotes the state of the believing man called forth by the divine acquittal."

Justification is the act of God removing from the sinner his guilt and the penalty incurred by that guilt, and bestowing a positive righteousness, Christ Jesus Himself in whom the believer stands, not only innocent and uncondemned, but actually righteous in point of law for time and for eternity. This is what God did for Abraham when he believed Him. This is what the Judaizers were attempting to merit for themselves by their own good works.

Translation. *Just as Abraham believed God, and his act of faith was credited to him, resulting in (his) righteousness.*

Verse seven. The words "know ye," are not imperative but indicative. "Ye perceive," is the sense. This verse contains a deduction from the previous verse. The word *therefore* from *ara,* is inferential. The argument is, "Since faith was the way Abraham was justified, it follows that those who exercise like faith, are his true followers." The word *faith* is here general in its application, indicating the determinative factor in life, as against works as a means of appropriating salvation. The expression "they which are of faith," refers to those who have exercised faith for salvation, and whose standing and character are consequently determined by that faith. The phrase "sons of Abraham," is not to be understood in a genealogical sense but rather in the ethical sense of the term. Abraham was accepted by God on the basis of faith, and God deals with all men on the same moral basis. God is no respecter of persons. Thus the faith exercised by Abraham is declared to be the fundamental condition of acceptance with God. *Children* is from *huioi,* properly *sons*.

Translation. *Ye perceive, therefore, that those who are of faith, these are sons of Abraham.*

Verse eight. This verse contains Paul's answer to the false assumption of the Judaizers that inasmuch as it is in Abraham that all nations were to be blessed, they would have to be incorporated in his descendants by the rite of circumcision.

GREEK NEW TESTAMENT

By the use of the word *and*, from *de*, Paul asserts that the blessing of Abraham, namely, the one he received from God, justification, was received by him through faith, and that it is through the exercise of a like faith that the Gentiles become his spiritual children, and not through submission to circumcision.

The expression *the scripture*, usually denotes a particular passage of scripture (see Luke 4:21; II Tim. 3:16). The passage referred to here is Genesis 12:3. Paul attributes foresight to scripture. This is a figure of speech expressing the thought that God's divine foresight is expresssed in the scriptures. The Jews had the formula, "What did the scripture foresee?"

Thus God, foreseeing that He would justify the Gentiles by faith announced the gospel to Abraham, which message was to be received by faith. The good news announced to Abraham was that some day the Saviour would arise out of his nation Israel, and that the Gentiles would be saved through Him as Abraham was saved. Thus, Abraham rejoiced to see the coming of that day (John 8:56). Abraham was therefore to become the pattern to all who would follow, of how a sinner, Jew or Gentile, must appropriate salvation. The words *would justify*, are from a present tense verb in Greek, the thought being that Paul is here dealing with a general principle, God's rule of action on the basis of which He operates for all time. Thus, the condition upon which any person was to be justified is faith, and this was announced to Abraham before he was circumcised, which means that circumcision had nothing to do with the acceptance of salvation.

Translation. *And the scripture forseeing that on a basis of faith God justifies the Gentiles, announced the gospel beforehand to Abraham, namely, All the Gentiles shall be blessed in you.*

Verse nine. This is a definite statement of the proposition which Paul wishes to prove. The emphasis is upon the fact that the believing ones are blessed with salvation, rather than those who depend upon good works as the Judaizers did. The word *faithful* is added as a descriptive word in order to impress upon the reader that the important thing about Abraham was the fact that he chose the faith way of salvation rather than depend upon personal merit and good works. The word here does not speak of faithfulness of life in the sense of fidelity, but of the fact that Abraham believed God. And well might Abraham have depended upon good works, from a purely human standpoint. Excavations in the city of Ur where Abraham lived, reveal the fact that Abraham was not a wild desert sheik, but an educated, wealthy, sophisticated citizen of the world, a man living in and ostensibly partaking of a state of culture and opulence little dreamed of by the person who is unfamiliar with the ancient civilizations of the past. Abraham was no ignoramus with a gullible faith. With all his cultural background, and in spite of it, he saw that much of that with which we have to do, is taken upon faith, including the way of salvation. Those who exercise a like faith to Abraham, share with him in the same salvation which he received from God.

Translation. *So that those who are believing ones are being blessed in company with believing Abraham.*

III. *The Judaizers taught that the law was a means of justification. But Paul shows that the law is a means of condemnation, and that it is the Lord Jesus who rescues us from its condemnation through the blood of His Cross* (3:10-14).

Verse ten. Paul quotes from Deuteronomy 27:26. Instead of being blessed by their act of putting themselves under the law, men put themselves under a curse. The Judaizers maintained that their knowledge of the law entitled them to the blessings which were attached to the sons of Abraham. Our Lord said to representatives of this same system: "Ye are constantly searching the scriptures;[17] and in them ye think ye have eternal life: and they are they which testify of Me. And ye will not come to Me that ye might have life" (John 5:39, 40). This was the sin of Israel, ignoring the righteousness of God, Christ, and going about to establish its own righteousness (Rom. 10:1-4). Paul argues that on the contrary, Israel has by its attempt to be justified by the law, entailed the curse of the broken law, for no man could keep

---

17. The verb is indicative, not imperative. They were searching the Scriptures,

the law. This curse is not merely the wrath of God in the form of the final banishment of the sinner from His presence, with all the sorrow and misery which that includes, but represents also a present condition of alienation from God caused by a violation of His law. The word *continueth* is a figurative expression. It speaks of the law as a prescribed district or domain in which one remains or out of which one goes.

Translation. *For as many as are of the works of the law, are under curse. For it stands written, Cursed is every one who is not remaining constantly in all things which stand written in the book of the law in order to do them.*

Verse eleven. The words "by the law" are in the Greek *en nomoi,* literally "in law," corresponding to "in the book of the law" of verse 10. We have here the locative of sphere. The man who does not continue in the sphere of the law is under the curse. And the man who attempts to remain in the sphere of the law by obeying it, is not justified in the sight of God, and for the reason that justification is by faith. The reason why obedience to the law cannot justify a sinner is that his obedience cannot pay for his sin. Only blood can pay for sin, for blood means outpoured death, and death is the wages of sin. God declares a believing sinner righteous on the basis of the fact that Christ has met the requirements of the law which we broke and Himself becomes our righteousness.

The word *just* as describing *man* is used as a legal rather than an ethical term. It refers to the man approved by God and accepted on the basis of faith, not to the man's character as exhibited by what he does. The words *shall live* refer as the context indicates, not to the impartation of a new and divine life which produces a new experience, but to the act of God in justifying him. He lives in a new relationship to God, that of being accepted in the Beloved.

Translation. *But that in a sphere of law no one is being justified in the sight of God is clear, because, The righteous man shall live by means of faith.*

Verse twelve. The statement, "The law is not of faith" means that the two principles of law and of faith as a means of justification are mutually exclusive of one another. They are diametrically opposed to each other. Then Paul quotes Leviticus 18:5, "The man that doeth them shall live in them." Light is thrown upon this statement by the apostle in Romans 10:5 where he quotes this same passage from Leviticus, when he says, "Moses describeth the righteousness which is of the law." That means that there is a righteousness that a human being could accrue to himself by a perfect obedience to the law, a thing which a fallen sinful human being cannot do, but which a perfect sinless being could do. But that righteousness would be different from the righteousness which God imputes to the believing sinner. The former would be obtained by works, and would be a human righteousness. The latter is obtained by faith and is a divine righteousness. Under the legal enactments of the Mosaic law, this could be the futile attempt of a sinner to work out under law a righteousness which God could approve. Under grace, it is the act of a believing sinner accepting as a gift, a righteousness which God has approved, even the Lord Jesus Himself.

Translation. *And the law is not of faith; but the one who has done them, shall live in them.*

Verse thirteen. The word *redeemed* is from *exagorazo,* the general significance of which is "to redeem from slavery." It means "to buy up." It is used frequently in the LXX, with the idea that such deliverance involves cost of some kind, effort, suffering, or loss to the one who effects the deliverance. It conveys the figure of a ransom. Men needed a ransom, for the law had left them prisoners under sentence of death.

There are three Greek words translated by the words *bought* or *redeemed.* These three tell the story of redemption. The first is *agorazo* (I Cor. 6:20), which means *to buy in the slave market.* We are slaves of sin. Our ransom price was paid by the Lord Jesus, His precious blood. Peter in his first epistle (1:18) says that we were not redeemed with little silver and gold coins used to buy a slave out of slavery, but with precious blood, highly honored, as of a lamb without spot or blemish, the blood of Christ. Thus, believers become bondslaves of the Lord Jesus by right of purchase. The word *doulos, bondslave*, translated *servants* in Romans 6:18, refers to one born in slavery.

The second word is the one Paul uses in the verse we are studying, *exagorazo, to buy a slave out of the market-place*. The bondslave of the Lord Jesus is bought not only to be His bondslave, but he is bought out of the slave market, never to be put up for sale in any slave market. He becomes the bondslave of the Lord Jesus for time and for eternity.

The third word is *lutroo* (I Peter 1:18; Titus 2:14). The noun having the same root means "ransom money used to liberate a slave." The verb means "to set free by the payment of a ransom." The bondslave of the Lord Jesus is set free from his former slavery to sin, to realize in his life that for which God created him, to glorify God and to enjoy Him forever.

The curse here is that which the legalistic passages of the Mosaic law pronounced upon those who did not perfectly obey its demands. The law pronounced a blessing and a curse. But the blessing proved barren, for the law made no allowance for human sin and frailty. The curse, which involved the wrath of a righteous God, brought condemnation upon the offender. From this hopeless state of condemnation in which the sinner was not only helpless to redeem himself, but helpless to satisfy the just demands of the law and thus find acceptance with God, Christ redeemed us by satisfying the just demands of the law which we broke, paying the penalty in our stead, leaving a holy God free to bestow mercy on the basis of justice satisfied.

A vivid picture of it all is given us in the three expressions, *under the curse* (3:10), *made a curse for (above) us* (3:13), and *redeemed us out from under the curse* (3:13). Sinners were under the curse. Christ came above us, thus between us and the curse. He took the blow of the Damascus blade that hung over us, and took us out from under the curse, having become a curse above us. The word *above* is the root meaning of *huper*, the preposition of substitution, used already in this epistle by Paul to speak of the substitutionary character of our Lord's death.

The word *us* refers to the Jewish nation. The Mosaic law was given to the Jew only. That is not to say however that the Gentile is not held responsible by God under the all-inclusive principles of right conduct that inhere in God's character and in His dealings with the human race. Thus the Jew was under the curse, and being redeemed by Christ from the curse, the blessing of Abraham, justification by faith, which in the plan of God was to flow through Israel to the Gentiles, was at liberty to flow out to the latter.

The words *being made* are from *genomenos* which means "to become." It is a participle of means, expressing the method by which Christ redeemed us from the curse. In the words "Cursed is everyone that hangeth on a tree," Paul is quoting from Deuteronomy 21:23. They are introduced by Paul to support his statement to the effect that Christ became a curse. The Deuteronomy passage has reference to the dead body of a criminal who had been put to death by stoning, and which was hung upon a tree. There is no reference here to Roman crucifixion, which was unknown at the time of Moses. Paul quotes from the LXX and omits the words *of God* after *cursed*, since our Lord was in no sense accursed by God in His crucifixion. It was the curse of the Mosaic law that descended on Christ, subjecting Him to the death of a malefactor. The law satisfied its demands upon the Lord Jesus, and thus thrust Him out of the pale of its legal jurisdiction. Believers, being identified with Him in His death in which He paid our penalty, are likewise cast out with Him, and are therefore no longer under curse.

Translation. *Christ delivered us by the payment of ransom from the curse of the law by becoming a curse in behalf of us, because it stands written, Accursed is every one who is suspended upon a tree.*

Verse fourteen. There are two purpose clauses in this verse, each introduced by the word *that* (*hina*). These are coordinate, depending upon the statement in verse 13 to the effect that Christ became a curse for us in order that the blessing of Abraham, justification by faith, and also the Holy Spirit, might be given to both Jew and Gentile (Joel 2:28). The law which was the barrier that separated Jew and Gentile, is done away in Christ. By its removal, the Gentiles are put on a common level with the Jew, and thus united, both Jew and Gentile are recipients of the Holy Spirit through faith.

Translation. *In order that to the Gentiles the blessing of Abraham might come in Jesus Christ; in order that the promise of the Spirit we (Jew and Gentile) might receive through faith.*

IV. *God made provision for justification to be given on the basis of faith in Jesus Christ to the Gentiles, and also the gift of the Spirit to both Jew and Gentile, doing this before the Mosaic law was given. The law therefore cannot make void that which was done by God prior to the giving of the law* (3:15-18).

Verse fifteen. Paul now presents an argument to show that the covenant God made with Abraham was still in force, basing it upon the priority of the covenant and its irrevocable character. He asserts that it is common knowledge that when men make a contract, and that contract is once agreed upon, it cannot be modified or changed except by the mutual consent of both parties to the contract. Paul applies this to God's covenant with Abraham, contending that the law cannot modify it since it was given centuries later.

Paul addresses them as brethren here. In the preceding section he was not so much addressing the Galatians as he was speaking of the Judaizers. Here he is directly addressing the former. It was an expression of loving urgency, and conciliatory in tone. How different is this from the apostle's abrupt "Paul . . . . . to the churches of Galatia" (1:1, 2).

The words, "I speak after the manner of men" have in them the idea of, "I speak from a human point of view," or, "I speak as men do concerning their affairs." Paul is not apologizing for the illustration he is using, but is desirous of accommodating himself to the ordinary way in which the average man thinks, so as to be perfectly intelligible to his readers.

The word translated *covenant,* deserves careful treatment. It is the word *diatheke* which in its verb form means "to place between two." It refers to the act of one of two individuals placing between them something to which he obligates himself. It is an engagement on the part of one in the sense that he enters into an agreement with another to do thus and so. The word here must not be understood as meaning a *testament*, namely, the testamentary disposition of goods. It is used only once in the New Testament in that way (Heb. 9:15-17). It refers to an agreement in which God enters into covenant relations with Abraham, and in which He promises to justify him on the basis of his faith in the atonement which He Himself would some day offer. That covenant or agreement was made by God. God also gave the law centuries later, and the God who made a covenant with Abraham would not invalidate that covenant by adding another specification to it, namely, obedience to law coupled with faith as the two prerequisites to salvation.

The word *confirmed* is from *kuroo* which means "to confirm solemnly or publicly, to ratify." It is in the perfect tense, which indicates that the ratification is a past matter, and that at present the matter is closed and established. Therefore, just as in human relations, an agreement solemnly ratified cannot be changed unless by mutual consent of the parties involved, so in this divine relationship. "No man disannuleth or addeth thereto." *Disannuleth* is from *atheteo* which means "to render without place or standing, to abrogate, to annul." *Addeth thereto* is from *diatasso*, which means, "to make additional prescriptions." Two distinct methods of invalidating a contract are, *first*, to annul it directly, and *second*, to impose new conditions which are diametrically opposed to its spirit or purpose. The doctrine of the Judaizers at first glance appeared only to add some harmless new conditions to the covenant of grace. *But the character of these new conditions virtually annulled it. Works added to faith would annul the entire covenant since any dependence upon works means that it is necessary to abandon faith. That means that any sinner who claims to be saved on the basis of works plus faith is still a lost sinner.* One cannot carry water on two shoulders. Neither can one depend upon self effort to save one, and at the same time put faith in the Lord Jesus for salvation.

Here is the terrible tragedy of those systems which teach that works are needed for salvation in addition to faith in the atoning sacrifice of the Lord Jesus. They are sending millions to the Lake of Fire by their heretical teaching.

Translation. *Brethren, what I have to say is in accordance with common human practice. Even though it be a man's covenant, when it has finally been ratified, no man annuls it nor adds stipulations to it.*

Verse sixteen. The promises were made to Abraham and to his seed, Christ. But when Christ is seen as seed of Abraham here, all those saved by Him are included. The word *seed* when used in the singular number in the Old Testament means *progeny*. Thus to Abraham personally and to all those who by faith in Christ are brought into salvation, were the promises made. *The fact that the promises were made to Abraham and to all believers all down the ages who follow Abraham in his act of faith, indicates that the faith way of salvation existed before the law was given, continued through the time the law was in force, and still is in effect after the abrogation of the law at the Cross. Thus the entrance of the law did not affect the covenant at all.*

Translation. *Now to Abraham were made the promises, and to his seed. He does not say, And to the seeds, as in respect to many (seeds), but in respect to one (seed), and to your seed who is Christ.*

Verse seventeen. The words "And this I say," take up for the purpose of further argument or explanation a thought which has already been expressed. In verse 16, Paul has by inference hinted at what he states plainly in this verse. The figure of 430 years, Paul probably took from Exodus 12:40. The statement of the length of time that elapsed between the giving of the covenant to Abraham and the giving of the law to Moses, implies that the law was something new and different which could not therefore be an element forming part of the promise. The longer the covenant was in force as the alone method upon which God operated in the saving of sinners, the more impressive is Paul's statement. God was saving men on the basis of faith without works since the time of Adam, or 2,500 years before the law was given. The law was in force from Moses to Christ, or for a period of 1500 years. At the Cross it was abrogated. The Judaizers not only attempted to retain the Mosaic institutions for the Jews, but tried to impose them upon the Gentiles, *to whom that law was never given*. This was what Paul was fighting.

Paul's argument therefore is as follows. If a covenant once in force cannot be changed or rendered void by any subsequent action, God's covenant with Abraham cannot be changed or rendered void by the subsequent law. If this principle holds good in a human covenant, much more is it true when God makes the covenant, since God is more certainly true to His promise than man.

Translation. *This now is what I mean. A covenant previously established by God,* [18] *the law, which came after four hundred and thirty years, does not render void, with the result that the promise becomes inoperative.*

Verse eighteen. Paul's argument in this verse is, that if the law affects the promise at all, it renders it null and void. It cannot be added to it without destroying it. Salvation must rest either upon the promise *or* upon the law. The Judaizers claimed that it rested upon the promise *and* the law. But Paul has shown that the law did not abrogate the promise, and thus it had no effect upon it. Thus, if as the Judaizers say, the inheritance is on the basis of law obedience, then it is not on the basis of promise. But, Paul adds, God gave it to Abraham on the basis of promise. That settled the matter. The words, *law* and *promise* are without the definite article, indicating that Paul is speaking of them here in their character of two opposing principles.

The word *gave* is from *charizomai*. This is a specialized word. It denotes not merely a gift, but a gift which is given out of the spontaneous generosity of the giver's heart, with no strings tied to it. The Greek word *grace* (*charis*) has the same root and the same meaning. Thus the word refers, not to an undertaking

---

18. The words "in Christ," are a rejected reading.

based upon terms of mutual agreement, but upon the free act of one who gives something, expecting no pay for it. This at once shows the difference between law and grace. If salvation were by obedience to the law, that would mean that it would be based upon a mutual agreement between God and the sinner whereby God would obligate Himself to give salvation to any sinner who would earn it by obedience to the law. But the very genius of the word *charizomai* militates against the teaching of the Judaizers, namely, that salvation is by works. There is a Greek word *huposchesis* which is used of an offer based upon the terms of a mutual agreement. But it is not used here.

Furthermore, the verb *gave* is in the perfect tense here, which tense speaks of a past completed act having present results. The past act of God giving the inheritance on the basis of a promise, has present results, present to the writer. God gave the inheritance to Abraham by promise 2000 B.C. The results of this act were still in existence in the century when Paul wrote. The law was given 1500 B.C., and the promise still held good after the law came and had been set aside.

Translation. *For if the inheritance is from law (as a method of divine dealing), no longer is it from promise (as a method of divine dealing). But to Abraham through the intermediate instrumentality of promise God has in grace freely bestowed it.*

V. *If the law was never given as a means whereby a sinner might be saved, why was it given, and for what purpose?* (3:19-4:7).

   1. *It was given to show man that sin is not a mere following of evil impulses, but a direct violation of the laws of God* (3:19-23).

Verse nineteen. Paul now proceeds to answer the argument that if the law was never given as a means of salvation, then that fact leaves the law without a reason for being. He asserts that the law was given because of transgressions. The words *because of* are from *charin*, which may have either a causal or a telic force. The context and also Paul's conception of the functions of the law indicate that the latter is its usage here. The word *telic* is from the Greek *telos* which means, "tending toward an end, purposive." Thus, the law was given for the purpose of transgressions.

The crux of the whole assertion is found in the distinctive meaning of the word translated *transgressions*. It is *parabasis*. The simple verb means "to step," the prefixed preposition, "beyond." It refers to the act of a person stepping beyond a fixed limit into forbidden territory. The word for *sin* is *hamartia* which meant in classical Greek "to miss the mark," and was used of a person who failed to hit a target. The verb was used in connection with a direct object *hodos* (road), in a sentence where someone missed the road. Thus, the word implies a deviation from the right course of action. But the word in the classics never had the idea of a willful transgression or overstepping of limitations with reference to conduct imposed by the deity.

The word *parabasis* when used of human conduct, indicates a violation of the rights of others, or of limitations imposed upon one. This word Paul now uses to indicate the purpose of the giving of the law. Before the law was given by Moses to Israel, the wrong doing of man was recognized as *hamartia*, sin, a deviation from the course of right conduct. But when the law was given, sin was seen to be, not merely the following of evil impulses, but the violation of explicit law. Thus, the exceeding sinfulness of sin was recognized by the human race, which otherwise might not have been evident. The law therefore was not given because of the *existence* of transgressions, but to show *hamartia* (sin) in its true light, an overstepping of what is right into the realm of what is wrong. This revelation of the true nature of sin, would cause man to fear God's wrath, which in turn would give strength to the weakness of man's moral sense and thus educate his conscience and make it more sensitive to sin. The particular phase of the Mosaic law here as well as throughout all of the Galatian letter is the purely mandatory statutes of "Thou shalt," and "Thou shalt not."

The law was given therefore to set the stamp of positive transgression upon already existing sin. It was not to give the knowledge of sin as sin, but to show that it was a violation of God's commandments.

The law was *added,* Paul says. The word *added* is from *prostithemi,* the simple verb meaning "to place," the prefixed preposition, "toward." It marks the law as supplementary to the covenant of grace, and therefore subordinate to it. Paul in Romans 5:20 says, "The law entered," (*pareiserchomai*), that is, came in alongside. It was not added to grace as an extra provision whereby a sinner might appropriate salvation, for it is diametrically opposed to grace. It was brought in alongside of grace as a measure to show sinners the real nature of their sin and thus their need of a Saviour who in infinite grace offers them a salvation free in answer to faith.

It was brought in alongside until the seed should come to whom the promise was made. Grace flowed full and free from Adam's time to Abraham's, and from Abraham's time to Moses', and from Moses' time to Paul's. And it flows full and free from Paul's time through the present, and will be in force as the only way in which God saves a sinner, until the Great White Throne. The law was merely in force from Moses' time to Christ's death on the Cross, and even while it was in force, God saved sinners by pure grace.

The covenant of promise is therefore of permanent validity, beginning before and continuing through the period of the law, and afterwards. The law was a temporary provision brought in alongside of grace to show sinners their need of grace, from Moses' time to the Cross.

The law was ordained by angels, Paul says. The New Testament refers three times to the interposition of angels in the giving of the law. In Acts 7:53 the fact is mentioned in order to enhance the authority of the law. In Hebrews 2:2 it is contrasted with God's revelation in His Son. Here it is contrasted with God's familiar intercourse with Abraham in which He spoke to Abraham, calling him His friend. At Sinai, the law was given through two intermediaries, angels and Moses. The people stood afar off. Grace says, "Come nigh," law says, "Stand off." The object of showing how the law was given, was to indicate the inferior and subordinate position of the law in comparison to the superior position held by grace. The promise was given direct to Abraham, the law through two intermediaries, angels and Moses. Paul shows that the law does not, as the Judaizers claim, have as direct and positive a relation to the divine plan of salvation as does the promise. He also shows that it is only of transitory significance, whereas the promise has an eternal value and meaning.

Translation. *What is then the significance of the law? For the sake of transgressions it was added, until there should come the Seed to whom the promise was made, having been promulgated by angels through the instrumentality of the hand of a mediator.*

Verse twenty. In this verse Paul shows that the promise is superior to the law, for the former was given directly from God to Abraham, whereas the latter was given to Israel by God through a mediator. We will examine the statement, "A mediator is not of one." The word *mediator* is from *mesites,* which in turn comes from *mesos* which means *middle,* the *midst.* Thus a mediator is one who intervenes between two, either to make or restore peace and friendship, to form a compact, or ratify a covenant. The word in the Greek text is preceded by the definite article, making the word generic in character. That is, Paul is not referring here to any particular mediator as Moses, but to the office of a mediator, and to mediators in general looked upon as a class of individuals. However, this generic statement is intended to be applied to Moses, the mediator referred to in verse 19. The word *one* is masculine in gender, and therefore is personal, referring to a person. That is, a mediator does not act simply in behalf of one person. The very genius of the word implies that the mediator stands "in the midst" of two or more persons, thus acts as a go-between. It is not that the mediator acts in behalf of a plurality of persons that constitute one party, but that there is a plurality of parties between which he acts. Thus the law is a contract between two parties. God gives the law through a mediator Moses, and man is obligated to obey it. God will bless man if he obeys, and will punish man if he disobeys. But the promise of free grace is not in the nature of a contract between two parties. God acts alone and directly when He promises salvation to anyone who will receive it by the outstretched hand of faith. There are no good works to be done by the sinner in order that he might merit that salvation. Grace is unconditional. There are no strings tied to it. God is One, that is, He acts alone without a mediator in respect to the promise of grace. Therefore grace is superior to law. In the case of the former, God spoke directly to Abraham. In the case of the latter, He spoke to Israel through a mediator, Moses. The dignity of the law is thus seen to be inferior to that of the promise.

Translation. *Now, the mediator is not (a go-between representing the interests) of one (individual), but God is one (individual).*

Verse twenty one. The apostle then asks the question, "Is the law then against the promises of God?" The answer is that the law and the promises are not in conflict because each has a distinct function. The law is a ministry of condemnation. The promises are a ministry of salvation. The law judges a person on the basis of obedience or disobedience. The promises judge man on a basis of faith. The law, whose ministry is one of condemnation, was not intended to express God's attitude towards man. God's attitude towards man is one of grace. The law is not the basis of God's judgment of man. A sinner who rejects Christ, goes to the Lake of Fire for all eternity, not because he has broken God's laws, for his sin is paid for. He goes to a lost eternity, because he rejects God's grace in the Lord Jesus. The law is a revelation of the sinner's legal standing, and as such condemns him. It cannot therefore justify him, as the Judaizers claim.

Law and grace are not in conflict, since they operate in different spheres. For instance, here is a father who has discovered that his son has disobeyed his commands. He calls the son's attention to the law which he broke, and pronounces him guilty. He uses this very sentence of guilty to bring the boy to see his misdemeanor in its true light. The son becomes repentant, and the father assures him of his forgiveness. The father is not in conflict with himself when using law to bring his son to a realization of the true nature of his disobedience, in order that he might repent and thus put himself in a position where the father can forgive him. God is not in conflict with Himself when He gives the law that man might come to see his sin as a transgression or violation of His holy will, which is the first step in his act of repentance and faith, and which latter is answered by God with the gift of eternal life.

Furthermore, no law could give eternal life. The wages of sin is death. The law demands of the sinner the death penalty, spiritual and physical death. The law will not accept the good works of a sinner in lieu of the death penalty. Only the precious blood of Jesus could satisfy the righteous demands of the broken law. Salvation therefore is by grace, since God the Son took the sinner's place on the Cross and offers salvation to the one who believes on Him.

Translation. *Is therefore the law against the promises of God? God forbid. For if a law had been given which was able to impart life, righteousness in that case would have been from the law.*

Verse twenty two. The word *scripture* in the singular number refers to a particular passage. Two Old Testament passages to which Paul probably has reference, are, Psalm 143:2, quoted in Galatians 2:16, and Deuteronomy 27:26, quoted in 3:10. The word *concluded* is from *sunkleio* which means "to shut up, to confine." Scripture in its divine utterances regarding the universality of sin, is spoken of as a jailer who shuts all up in sin as in a prison. The function of the law was therefore to convict of sin that men might turn to the Lord Jesus for salvation.

Translation. *But the scripture shut up all under sin, in order that the promise on the ground of faith in Jesus Christ might be given to those who believe.*

Verse twenty three. The correct understanding of the expression, "Before faith came" is found in the fact that the definite article is used before the word *faith,* namely, "before the faith came." The article here identifies the faith mentioned in this verse with the faith spoken of in verse 22, personal faith in Jesus Christ as Saviour, exercised in this Age of Grace. That faith is fundamentally alike so far as its character goes, to the faith Abraham exercised, but different in that it looks back to an accomplished salvation at the Cross, whereas the faith of Abraham looked forward to the accomplishment of that salvation at Calvary. The former is faith in an historic Christ, whereas the latter was faith in a prophetic Christ. Faith has been the appointed means of obtaining the salvation of God since Adam's time. Faith itself did not begin to be exercised on the occasion of the Cross. Faith as such did not come then. But the particular faith in Jesus Christ as exercised in this Age of Grace came at the beginning of the age.

The word *kept* is from *phroureo,* which means "to keep in ward under lock and key." The law was a jailer who held in custody those who were subjected to sin, in order that they should not escape the consciousness of their sins and their liability to punishment. The word *unto* is from *eis,* and is not temporal in its significance, having the idea of *until,* but means here "with a view to." That is, sinners were kept guarded under the law with a view to their exercising faith in Christ. The law shut them up to one avenue of escape, namely, faith in Christ, for during the 1500 years in which the law was in force, it was the means of convicting sinners of their sins and of causing them to look ahead in faith to the atonement God would some day offer which would pay for their sins. These sinners were saved by the blood of Christ just as surely and just as eternally as believing sinners since the Cross. But when the faith in an historic Christ came, that is, a faith exercised in the Christ of history rather than in the Christ of prophecy, then the law was abrogated.

Translation. *But before the aforementioned faith came, under law we were constantly being guarded, being shut up with a view to the faith about to be revealed.*

2. *The law was given in order that, by showing the sinner that sin was an actual transgression of God's laws, he might see the necessity of faith in a substitutionary sacrifice for sin, and thus be led to put his trust in the Christ of prophecy who would in the future die for him (3:24-29).*

Verse twenty four. The word translated *schoolmaster* is the important word here. It is *paidagogos*. The word *schoolmaster* could better be the translation of *didaskalos* which means "a teacher." It is true that our word *pedagogue* comes from the Greek *paidagogos*, and that it refers to a schoolmaster. But the Greek word did not have that meaning. The word designated a slave employed in Greek and Roman families who had general charge over a boy in the years from about 6-16. He watched over his outward behavior, and took charge over him whenever he went from home, as for instance, to school. This slave was entrusted with the moral supervision of the child. His duties were therefore quite distinct from those of a schoolmaster. Furthermore, the metaphor of a *paidagogos* seems to have grown out of the word *kept* (*phroureo*) of verse 23, which means "to guard." Thus the word refers to a guardian of a child in its minority rather than to a teacher or schoolmaster.

By describing the law as a *paidagogos*, Paul emphasizes both the inferiority of the law to grace, and its temporary character. The law was therefore the guardian of Israel, keeping watch over those committed to its care, accompanying them with its commands and prohibitions, keeping them in a condition of dependence and restraint, and continually revealing to them sin as a positive transgression.

Translation. *So that the law became our guardian until Christ, in order that on the grounds of faith we might be justified.*

Verse twenty five. The article appears before the word *faith* in the Greek text, showing that it is the faith in the historic Christ which is referred to, as in verses 22 and 23.

Translation. *But (this) faith having come, no longer are we under the guardian.*

Verse twenty six. By the change from the first person *we,* with its reference to the Jews, to the second person *ye* with its reference to his readers, both Jew and Gentile, Paul shows that the wall of separation between Jew and Gentile had been broken down at the Cross, and that both Jew and Gentile become children of God in Christ Jesus. The word translated *children* is *huios* and is the important word here. This word signifies someone of full age. Under law, the individual was in his minority and under a guardian. Now, under grace, he has attained his majority, having outgrown the surveillance of his former guardian.

The context shows that the words "in Christ Jesus," must be separated from the words "by faith." They are put at the end of the sentence so as to form a distinct proposition which Paul enlarges upon in the following verses.

Translation. *For all of you are God's sons through faith, in Christ Jesus.*

Verse twenty seven. Having spoken of the Galatians in the previous verse as *in Christ,* referring to that mystical and vital union which exists between the Lord Jesus and the believer, Paul now reminds them of how they became united with Christ. When they put their faith in Him as Saviour, the Holy Spirit baptized (introduced or placed) them into vital union with Christ (Rom. 6:3; I Cor. 12:13). The reference cannot be to water baptism, for that never put a believing sinner in Christ. The Greek word *baptizo* means "to put or place into."[19]

The words *put on* are from *enduno.* The latter is used in the LXX, of the act of clothing one's self with strength, righteousness, glory, salvation. The word does not convey the idea of putting on a mask or playing the part of another. It refers to the act in which one enters into actual relationship with someone else. Chrysostom says, "If Christ is Son of God, and thou hast put Him on, having the Son in thyself and being made like unto Him, thou hast been brought into one family and one nature."

---
19. *Treasures,* pp. 84-87.

Translation. *For as many as were introduced into (a mystical union with) Christ, put on Christ.*

Verse twenty eight. The individual differences between Jew and Greek, between slave and free, between male and female, are merged in that higher unity into which all believers are raised by the fact that they all have a common life in Christ Jesus. One heart now beats in all. The pulsating life of the Lord Jesus is the motive power. One mind guides all, the mind of Christ. One life is lived by all, the life of the Lord Jesus produced by the Holy Spirit in the various circumstances and relations of each individual believer's experience.

Translation. *There is neither Jew nor Greek, there is neither slave nor free, there is neither male nor female. For ye are all one in Christ Jesus.*

Verse twenty nine. The Judaizers taught that by becoming subjects of the Mosaic law, the Galatian Gentiles would become the seed or progeny of Abraham. Paul asserts that this privilege comes to one by faith in Christ. In Romans 4, Paul shows that Abraham was justified by faith, and was thus constituted the spiritual father of all who put their faith in Christ, whether they are circumcised or uncircumcised. God made salvation dependent upon faith in order that it might be available to both Jew and Gentile. Since Abraham is the spiritual father of all believers, this does away with the false Jewish notion that kinship to Abraham brings one into the divine favor and gives one salvation. By belonging to Christ, believers are also Abraham's posterity, for Christ is the seed of Abraham. Since believers have entered into relationship with Christ, they must consequently have a share in the same state, and must likewise be Abraham's seed.

Translation. *And since ye are Christ's, then are ye Abraham's seed, heirs according to the promise.*

3. *It was given because the sinner is like a child in its minority, and can only be dealt with in a most elementary way (4:1-7).*

Verses one and two. Paul here continues the argument for the inferiority of the condition under law, using an illustration from contemporary life. In order to understand his argument, we must understand the technical terms which he uses. The first word is *child,* the translation of *nepios.* The Greek word is made up of two words that together mean "one that does not speak." The word refers to an immature person, intellectually and morally. This word Paul uses to describe the person under the law. He is treated as an immature person. An adult for instance, is old enough to govern his own actions. A child must have restraints put upon him. So in the spiritual world. Israel under law was treated like a minor. The word *servant* is the next term. The Greek word here is *doulos,* speaking of a bondslave. It is the term used of a slave in a servile condition. The minor was legally in much the same position as a slave. He could not perform any act except through his legal representative. This person was the guardian in the case of a minor, whose sanction was necessary for the validity of any contract undertaken in his behalf. The word *lord* is from *kurios,* which here is used in the sense of *owner.* The word *tutor* is from *epitropos,* the word which designates the guardian of a minor orphan. The word *governor* is from *oikonomos,* referring to a steward of one's property. The tutor was the guardian of the child's person, the governor, the guardian of the child's property. The words "the time appointed," are from *prothesmias,* an Athenian legal term referring to an appointed time for the termination of the minority, this time set by the father of the child. There is an illustration of this in the case of Antiochus Ephiphanes who appointed Lysias to be steward of the affairs of the kingdom and guardian of his son Antiochus Eupator until a specified time, that time being when the father would resume the authority on his return.

Translation. *Now I say, that as long as the heir is in his minority, he does not differ one bit from a slave, even though he is owner of all, but is under guardians and stewards until the time previously fixed by his father.*

Verse three. The word *we* refers to Christians, Gentile and Jew. *Children* is from *nepios,* the word meaning *immature,* thus, "when we were immature ones." *Elements* is from *stoicheion,* which refers to any first thing from which the others belonging to some series or composite whole take their rise. The word refers to first principles. The word *world* is from *kosmos* and is to be understood as in John 3:16; I Corinthians 6:2, 11:32, the world of humanity. The "elements of the world" refer here therefore to the first principles of non-Christian humanity; in the case of the Jew, to the symbolic and ceremonial character of Judaism and its legal enactments, and in the case of the Gentiles, to the ceremonial and ritualistic observances of the pagan religions.

Translation. *In like manner, we also, when we were in our minority, were in a permanent state of servitude under the rudimentary first principles of mankind.*

Verse four. In the phrase, "the fullness of the times," the words, "of the times" are in a construction called the objective genitive, in which the word "times" receives the action of the noun of action. The word *times,* (chronos), refers merely to time as conceived of as a succession of moments. The other Greek word for *time, kairos,* refers to the critical epoch-making periods foreordained by God. But the word Paul uses here refers merely to the lapse of time. The meaning is that when that moment came which completed the period of time designated by God that should elapse before the coming of the Son of God in incarnation, then He would send forth His Son.

This point of time marked some outstanding events in the history of the human race. *First,* it was the moment which God had ordained for Messiah's coming. To Daniel was given the date of His coming, 483 years after the edict of the Medo-Persian government to rebuild Jerusalem. *Second,* the Mosaic law had done its educational work, showing to the world that the most highly-favored nation on earth, the Jewish nation, was, despite all of God's blessings and mercy, totally depraved, giving the Gentile portion of the race a picture of its own totally depraved heart. *Third,* the Mosaic law in its three sections, the ten commandments, the laws governing social relationships, and the Levitical system of sacrifices, was done away with as a legal system, to be superseded by the gospel of grace centering faith in an historic Saviour. *Fourth,* the Roman empire maintained world peace. Roman roads made travel for missionaries easy. The universal use of the Greek language made the speedy propagation of the gospel possible. The earth-stage was all set for the greatest event in the history of the human race, the incarnation, sacrificial death, and bodily resurrection of God the Son.

The word translated *sent forth* demands study. It is *exapostello*. The word *apostello* refers to the act of one who sends another with a commission to do something, the person sent being given credentials. Our word *apostle* comes from it. The prefixed preposition *apo* means *from, off*. This means that the person sent is to represent the sender. He is his ambassador. Our Lord is called the Apostle and High Priest of our confession in Hebrews 3:1. But not only was our Lord sent off from the presence of the Father, but as the other prefixed preposition *ex* signifies, He was sent out from His presence. "Out from the ivory palaces, into a world of woe" came our Saviour.

Not only was He sent forth from Heaven, but He became incarnate in the human race through virgin birth, as the words "made of a woman" indicate. Not only did He become incarnate, but He was born and lived His life previous to His Cross under the Mosaic law, yes, under law as such, for the definite article is absent before the word *law* in the Greek text. He was subject to the Jewish legal economy just as any Jew was subject to it.

Translation. *But when there came the fulness of the time, God sent off His Son, woman born, made subject to law.*

Verse five. The word *redeem* is from *exagorazo* "to buy out of the slave market." The word *law* is not preceded by the definite article, hence law in general is referred to here. Paul conceived of the Gentiles as possessing a law, and that law being of divine origin. He speaks of the law written in the hearts of the Gentiles (Rom. 2:14, 15). This law written upon the Gentile heart could easily become externalized and be made into a legalistic system. In I Corinthians 9:20, Paul refers first to the Jews, and then to those who are under the law, including in the second expression, anyone who was living under a system of legalism, Jew or Gentile.

The Lord Jesus was born under the law, lived under the law, and died under the penalty of the law which we broke, and in paying our penalty, He delivered us from any claims which the law had against us. He died under law, and in His resurrection, was raised into a realm where law as a legalistic system does not exist. This He did, in order that He might not only deliver us from the law but also raise believers with Himself into a realm where law does not operate. Instead therefore of being children (immature ones, *nepios*) under law, we became adult sons (*huios*) under grace. We received the adoption of sons. This expression in the Greek is literally, " in order that we might receive the adult son-placing." We could paraphrase it "in order that we might be placed as adult sons." Thus, we have presented to us the status of a person under grace as compared to that of a person under law. The latter is in his minority, the former in his majority, the latter treated like a minor, the former like an adult.

Translation. *In order that He might deliver those under law, in order that we might receive the placing as adult sons.*

Verse six. The phrase "because ye are sons," gives the reason for God's act of sending the Holy Spirit to take up His permanent residence in the hearts of the Galatians. The act of the Spirit in placing the Galatian believers as adult sons of God, is the first and objective step which the preceding context has spoken of. This brought about their release from the position of minors under law, and placed them in the position of adult sons. The bestowal of the Holy Spirit gave the Galatians a consciousness of the filial relationship between themselves as sons of God and God their Father. Instead of looking upon God as a Judge, they could now look upon Him as their Father with whom they have the privilege of living as His sons. The fact of their possession of the indwelling Spirit was enough to demonstrate to the Galatians that they were no longer under law, but under grace.

The word *crying,* from *krazo,* signifies "a loud and earnest cry," or "a public announcement." See Matthew 9:27, Acts 14:14, Romans 9:27, John 7:28, 37. In the LXX it is often used of prayer addressed to God (Ps. 3:4, 107:13). It emphasizes the earnestness and intensity of the Holy Spirit's utterance in the Christian. The word itself does not convey the idea of joy, but the intensity of the Spirit's utterance in this case must include a joyous note. The word *crying* is, in the Greek text, associated with the word *Spirit,* so that it is the Spirit who is doing the crying.

He cries *Abba.* The word *pater* (father) is the Greek equivalent of the Aramaic word *Abba.* Aramaic is the language which the Jews spoke in Palestine in the first century. Paul translates the word *Abba* for his Greek readers who were not acquainted with Aramaic. It is possible that the use of the name *Abba* was derived from the Lord Jesus. When reporting in Greek the word Jesus used, His hearers would use the Aramaic *Abba* with a sort of affectionate fondness as the very term Jesus used to express the wonderful thought of filial relationship to God.

Translation. *And because you are sons, God sent forth the Spirit of His Son into your hearts crying Abba, my Father.*

Verse seven. In the fact of the Galatian's possession of the Spirit, Paul finds the proof that they are adult sons of God. The emphasis is still upon the fact that their position as sons gives them freedom from bondage to the law, for he says that they are no longer slaves (*doulos*). It is also implied by the use of the words "no longer," that at one time the Galatians were under bondage to law. The change from the plural *sons* to the singular *son* brings the matter of sonship closer home to each individual reader.

As a son, Paul says, the believer is an heir of God. The purpose of the apostle in again bringing up the conceptions of heirship and inheritance is perhaps that he wants to remind the Galatians that their position as heirs of God is due, not to any personal merit or good works, but to the grace of God. Thus, the Galatians are reminded that it is not through coming under law, but in maintaining their freedom from it that they will be able to obtain the blessing of Abraham, which blessing the Judaizers had held before their eyes as a prize obtainable only through circumcision. Paul appeals to them to retain the status of adult sons under grace which they already possessed, rather than go back to the position of a minor and a slave under law.

Translation. *So that no longer are you a slave but a son, and since (you are) a son, (you are) also an heir through God.*[20]

VI. *Yet the Galatians are determined to return to their former position as minors and slaves under law* (4:8-11).

Verse eight. The apostle speaks of the former gods which the Galatian Gentiles worshipped (Acts 14:9-18). He thinks of them as realities, calling the gods of the pagan world *demons* (I Cor. 8:5, 6, 10:19, 20; Col. 2:15). The words "did service" are from *douloo,* the kindred verb to *doulos,* a slave. The Galatians were slaves of these deities, in bondage under a system of legalism.

He grants them objective existence, but denies that they are gods by nature. The word *nature* is from *phusis* which means, "that which belongs to a person or thing by virtue of its origin," then, "its essential character." It is used even of the divine nature which is without origin. Paul does not deny their existence, but their deity. Yet while the apostle did not think of them as deity by nature, yet at the same time he did not class them as being of mere mundane matter. They belonged to a world not human but demoniac, a point which must have been well known to the Galatians from Paul's oral instruction.

Translation. *But at that time in fact, not knowing God, ye were in a slave's bondage to the gods which are not gods by nature.*

Verse nine. The expression "known by God," cannot refer merely to knowledge simply in a purely theocratic or intellectual sense, since the apostle must have regarded such knowledge by God as an ever present fact. The phrase must refer to God knowing the Galatians in a saving way. For this use see Psalm 1:6, Nahum 1:7, I Corinthians 8:3, Matthew 7:23. Paul adds the phrase, "or rather are known of God" to the phrase "after that ye have known God," for the following reasons. It is to remind the Galatians that they do not owe their knowledge of God to themselves, but to Him. Their escape from idolatry and bond-

---

20. The words "through Christ" are a rejected reading.

age to law was not effected by any knowledge they acquired of God, but by God coming to know them in a saving way. Hence, they should clearly see the folly and wrong of abandoning this advantageous position to take an inferior one from which they had been rescued. *Eadie* says in this connection, "God knew them ere they knew Him, and His knowing them was the cause of their knowing Him." Dean Stanley remarks that "Our knowledge of God is more His act than ours." If God knows a man, that means that an activity of God has passed over to man, so that the man, as the subject of God's knowledge, enters into the knowledge of God. The Greek word translated *know* here is *ginosko*, which in the New Testament often implies a personal relation between the knower and the known.

The word *how* is from *pos,* rather, "how is it possible?" It is, as Bengel says, a question full of wonder. The apostle could hardly conceive of such a thing as a believer, having been once rescued from abject slavery to demons in a pagan religion, returning to a human system of bondage. The word *turn* is present in tense, "How is it possible that you are turning?" They were in the act of turning away from grace to law while Paul was writing this letter.

The question, "How is it possible that you are turning back again to the weak and beggarly rudimentary things to which ye desire to be in bondage again?" is a rhetorical one, the purpose of which is to show the absurdity of their actions. It also calls the attention of the Galatians to the ineffectualness and poverty of their old religious system, contrasted to the power and richness of the gospel. It is of course a perverted form of Judaism to which they were turning, but pagan religions are included in Paul's thought as just as ineffectual. Both were legalistic in character, and were without a dynamic to make actual the realization of ethical principles in the life.

The words *again* are from *palin* and *anothen* respectively, Greek synonyms meaning *again.* The first refers to a repetition of an act. The second speaks of the repetition of an act, that repetition having the same source as the first act. In other words, in the second word there is a return to a former position. The Galatians, in turning to a system of legalism, would be returning to their former position under law. The word *anothen* not only refers to the act of returning to a former position, but of returning to the beginning. These Galatians would be going back to the elementary beginning principles of religious thought.

When Paul speaks of the rudimentary forms of religion, calling them weak and beggarly, he shows the utter impotence of these to do and bestow what was done and bestowed by God in grace. They are weak in that they have no power to rescue men from condemnation. They are beggarly, since they bring no rich endowment of spiritual blessings.

Up to this point, Paul has spoken with respect to the education given to the world by the social habits, institutions, and laws of the Greco-Roman world. Through this education, civilized man learnt much in the sphere of morals and natural religion which would bear comparison with the progress of Israel under the ethics of the Mosaic law. But when he compares the mechanical routine of formal religious ceremonies which were found in the pagan religions and among so-called religious Jews, with the spiritual teachings and dynamics of the gospel, he does not hesitate to call them weak and beggarly. *Lightfoot* has a most illuminating note on this matter which is so valuable that we quote it in its entirety.

"It is clear however from the context, that the apostle is not speaking of the Jewish race alone, but of the heathen world also before Christ — not of the Mosaic law only, but of all forms of law which might be subservient to the same purpose. This appears from his including his Galatian hearers under the same tutelage. Nor is this fact to be explained by supposing them to have passed through a stage of Jewish proselytism on their way to Christianity. St. Paul distinctly refers to their previous idolatrous worship (verse 8), and no less distinctly and emphatically does he describe their adoption of Jewish ritualism, as a *return* to the weak and beggarly discipline of childhood, from which they had been emancipated when they abandoned that worship.

"But how, we may ask, could St. Paul class in the same category that divinely ordained law which he elsewhere describes as 'holy' and 'just' and 'good' (Rom. 7:12), and those degraded heathen systems which he elsewhere reprobates as 'fellowship with devils'[21] (I Cor. 10:20)?

"The answer seems to be that the apostle here regards the higher elements in heathen religions as corresponding, however imperfectly, to the lower element in the Mosaic law. For we may consider both the one and the other as made up of two component parts, the *spiritual* and the *ritualistic*.

"Now viewed in their *spiritual* aspect, there is no comparison between the one and the other. In this respect the heathen religions, so far as they added anything of their own to that sense of dependence upon God which is innate in man and which they could not entirely crush (Acts 14:17, 17:23, 27 and 28; Rom. 1:19 and 20), were wholly bad; they were profligate and soul-destroying, were the prompting of devils. On the contrary, in the Mosaic law, the spiritual element was most truly divine. But this does not enter into our reckoning here, for Christianity has appropriated all that was spiritual in its predecessor. The Mosaic dispensation was a foreshadowing, a germ of the gospel: and thus, when Christ came, its spiritual element was of necessity extinguished or rather absorbed by its successor. Deprived of this, it was a mere mass of lifeless ordinances, differing only in degree, not in kind, from any other ritualistic system.

"Thus the *ritualistic* element alone remains to be considered, and here is the meeting point of Judaism and Heathenism. In Judaism this was as much lower than its spiritual element, as in Heathenism it was higher. Hence the two systems approach within such a distance of each other that they can under certain limitations be classed together. They have at least so much in common that a lapse into Judaism can be regarded as a relapse to the position of unconverted Heathenism. Judaism was a system of bondage like Heathenism. Heathenism had been a disciplinary training like Judaism.

---

21. The word is *daimonion*, referring to demons. See *Nuggets*, p. 104.

"It is a fair inference, I think, from St. Paul's language here, that he does place Heathenism in the same category with Judaism in this last respect. Both alike are *stoicheia,* 'elementary systems of training.' They had at least this in common, that as ritual systems they were made up of precepts and ordinances, and thus were representatives of 'law' as opposed to 'grace,' 'promise,' that is, as opposed to the gospel. Doubtless in this respect the highest form of heathen religion was much lower and less efficient than the Mosaic ritual. But still in an imperfect way they might do the same work: they might act as a restraint which, multiplying transgressions, and thus begetting and cherishing a conviction of sin, prepared the way for the liberty of manhood in Christ."

Translation. *But now having come to know God, indeed rather having become known by God, how is it possible that you are turning back again to the weak and beggarly rudimentary principles to which ye are bent on again being in bondage?*

Verse ten. The days, months, and years which the Galatians were observing, were those which the Mosaic law required Israel to observe. This is made clear by Paul's statement in 4:21, to the effect that the Galatians are bent on being under law. From 5:1 it is clear that the Galatians had not yet adopted circumcision, and from 5:3, that they had not been asked to adopt the whole law as yet. This shows that the Judaizers had pursued the adroit course of presenting to them only part of the requirements of the Mosaic law, those parts which might be least repulsive to them as Gentiles. Having gotten them to adopt the festivals and perhaps the fast days, the Judaizers were now urging them to adopt circumcision.

The word *observe* is from *paratereo*. The word denotes careful, scrupulous observance, an intent watching lest any of the prescribed seasons be overlooked. A merely legal or ritualistic system of religion always develops such scrupulousness. Paul, a former Pharisee, was well acquainted with the meticulous care with which the Pharisees kept all the appointed feasts and fasts. It hurt him to see these Gentile Christians being drawn into the net of the Judaizers, and enslaved by a mere formal, lifeless ritual.

The *days* probably refer to the Sabbath days and to the feasts which were observed just for a day. The *months* refer to the monthly recurring events (Isaiah 66:23), or to the seventh month (Numbers 29). The reference also could have to do with the celebration of the appearance of the new moon (Numbers 10:10, 28:11). *Times* refers to the celebrations not limited to a single day, such as the Passover, Feast of Tabernacles, and to the feasts of the fourth, fifth, and seventh months (II Chron. 8:13). *Years* may have reference to the year of Jubilee or the Sabbatical year.

Translation. *Days ye are scrupulously and religiously observing, and months, and seasons, and years.*

Verse eleven. Martin Luther said of this verse, "These words of Paul breathe tears." The construction in the Greek does not give the impression that the apostle has fears about the future of the Galatians which may not be realized. It is clear that he suspects that what he fears has already happened. Paul was not apprehensive with respect to his own interests or his fruitless labors, but with respect to the spiritual welfare of his Galatian converts. They were the objects of his anxiety.

The word *labour* is from *kopiao* which means "to labor to the point of exhaustion." It is in the perfect tense, indicating the finished, thorough piece of work Paul had done in the evangelization of the Galatians.

Translation. *I am afraid about you lest perhaps in vain I have labored to the point of exhaustion for you.*

VII. *Paul appeals in a touching way to the Galatians to maintain their freedom from the law. He reminds them of their enthusiastic reception of him and the gospel which he preached, and tells them of his longing to be with them now in order that he might speak to them personally* (4:12-20).

Verse twelve. He exhorts them, "Be as I am, for I am as ye are." The word "be" is from *ginomai* which means literally "to become." His exhortation is therefore, "Become as I am, because I also became as you are." That is, "become as I am, free from the bondage of the law. I became as you are, Gentile." Paul exhorts the Galatians to free themselves from bondage to law as he had done. He appeals to them to do this because he who had possessed the advantages of the law, had foregone these advantages and had placed himself on the same level in relation to the law as Gentiles. He tells them that he gave up all those time-honored Jewish customs and those dear associations of race to become like them. He has lived like a Gentile so that he might preach to Gentiles. He pleads with them not to abandon him when he has abandoned all for them.

The Galatians could not fail to remember the occasion when at the close of Paul's address at Pisidian Antioch, the Jews departed from the synagogue, but the Gentiles besought him to repeat to them the words of life on the next Sabbath. They could not fail to remember how the Jews had expelled Paul from the city. They, the Galatian Gentiles, had been suitors to Paul to maintain the freedom of the gospel. Now, he in turn is appealing to *them* to maintain the freedom of that same gospel.

Translation. *Become as I am, because I also became as you were, brethren, I am beseeching you. Ye had done me no wrong.*

Verse thirteen. Paul reminds the Galatians of the fact that when he came to Antioch the first time, it was not his intention to evangelize that territory, but to go on to another place, and that a sudden attack of illness made it imperative that he stay there. Thus it was because of his illness, that he preached the gospel to them.

Regarding Paul's illness at Antioch, the following facts should be noted. *First,* it occurred under the observation of the Galatians who watched its progress, were familiar with its repulsive symptoms, and showed tender sympathy toward the sufferer. This fact may help us to understand the words, "Ye had done me no wrong." The Galatians might easily have spurned Paul and refused his fellowship. There he was, a Jew, and a stranger to them, afflicted with an illness that normally aroused disgust and loathing by reason of its repulsive nature. But instead of doing Paul the wrong of rejecting him, they welcomed him with open arms, and his gospel message with open hearts. *Second,* the Galatians knew that Paul had not intended to work among them. His face was turned to the Greek cities of Asia Minor and the mainland of Greece itself. They knew that he was detained amongst them by his illness. *Third*, this illness which incapacitated him for further travel, yet allowed free intercourse with those around him. *Fourth*, the success he had in winning the Galatians to the Lord Jesus, indicates that his illness was of a chronic nature. His sick chamber was his pulpit. *Fifth*, in connection with his reference to his illness, Paul mentions the fact in verse 15 that if it had been possible, the Galatians would have plucked out their eyes and would have given them to him. The inference should be clear that he needed a new pair of eyes, and that therefore his illness was an eye affliction. His words in 6:1, "Ye see with what large letters I have written to you with my own hand," confirm this, the large Greek letters being necessary because of his impaired vision. A further confirmation of this is found in the fact that in the lowlands of Pamphylia, a region through which Paul had just passed on his way to Pisidian Antioch, an oriental eye disease called ophthalmia was prevalent. In addition to all this, the Greek words translated *despised* and *rejected*, indicate that the illness had caused him to have a repulsive appearance, which answers to the symptoms of *ophthalmia*.

Translation. *But ye know that because of an infirmity of the flesh, I preached the gospel to you on the occasion of my first visit.*

Verse fourteen. The best Greek texts read *your*, referring to the Galatians, not *my*, referring to Paul. Paul's illness was in a sense a temptation to the Galatians, in that its nature was such that a normal reaction to it would be in the form of loathing and disgust, which attitudes would be followed by the rejection of the afflicted one. The word *despised* is from *ekptuo* which means "to spit out, to reject, to spurn, to loathe." *Rejected* is from *exoutheneo* which means "to hold and treat as of no account, to despise." There was something in the physical appearance of the apostle that tempted the Galatians to reject him and his message.

Instead of spurning Paul, these unsaved Galatians had received him as an angel of God, even as Jesus Christ. The reference is probably to the occasion of the healing of the lame man at Lystra. In their excitement at this miraculous healing, the Lycaonians thought that Barnabas was Zeus, the chief of the Greek gods, and that Paul was Hermes, the messenger and the interpreter of the gods. Paul looks back to the day when these Galatians had received him as a messenger of the gods, even as the son of God. This was, to be sure an outburst of native superstition and pagan religion, and was repudiated at the time with indignation by Paul. However, these converted Galatians could look back at all this and thank God with a feeling of grateful joy that they had not welcomed the Greek gods of Olympus, but messengers of the living God who had made heaven and earth. There is an echo of this same incident in Paul's words in 1:8, "But though we or an angel from heaven preach any other gospel unto you than that we have preached unto you."

Translation. *And the temptation to which ye were subjected and which was in my flesh, ye did not loathe nor utterly despise, but as a messenger of God ye received me, as Christ Jesus.*

Verse fifteen. The word *blessedness* is from *makarios* which in secular Greek means *prosperous,* and which indicates that the *makarios* person is in a state of prosperity. Paul reminds the Galatians of the prosperity of their spiritual lives which consisted of such a state of self-sacrifice and self-abnegation that they were willing to dig out their own eyes and give them to Paul. He asks, Where is that prosperous condition now?

The reader should know that the author has not followed *Burton, Vincent, Lightfoot, Meyer,* and *Alford* on the question of the nature of Paul's illness, but instead, the *Rev. Frederic Rendall,* in *Expositor's Greek Testament,* and *Dr. A. T. Robertson.* However, the decision of the writer is not based simply nor primarily upon the authority of the last two men named. That which tipped the scales in favor of the *ophthalmia* solution, was the Greek text of 4:13-15 and 6:11. Let the reader judge for himself as to whether the evidence presented is conclusive.

Translation. *Where is therefore your (spiritually) prosperous state? For I bear witness to you that if it had been possible, you would have dug out your own eyes and would have given them to me.*

Verse sixteen. Therefore is from *hoste,* which is often used by Paul in the sense of *therefore,* to introduce an imperative or an affirmative conclusion but not an interrogation. The word enemy is from *echthros* which speaks of an enemy in an active sense, of one who is hostile to another. Paul says that he has become an enemy of the Galatians, not from his point of view, but from the standpoint of the Galatians. He refers to the fact that he has told them the truth. It was probably on the occasion of his second visit to them (Acts 18:23) that he found the danger impending, and spoke plainly against the Judaizers.

Translation. *So then I have become your enemy because I am telling you the truth.*

Verse seventeen. In contrast to his own frank truthfulness in which he risked incurring the displeasure of the Galatians, the apostle tells them of the Judaizers' dishonorable attempt at paying them court in order to win them over to themselves. The word they refers to the Judaizers. The fact that Paul does not mention the Judaizers by name, is in keeping with the emotional strain and the irritation he was experiencing at the time. Calvin says, "For those whom it disgusts and offends us to mention, we generally refer to with a suppression of the name." The words "zealously affect" are from *zeloo.* The word *affect* as used here, is an example of one of the obsolete words in the Authorized Version. The word is from *affectaire* which means "to strive after, to earnestly desire." Shakespeare in *The Taming of the Shrew* has, "In brief, sir, study what you most affect." Ben Jonson has, "Pray him aloud to name what dish he affects." Chaucer gives us, "As Crossus dide for his affectis wronge" (his wrong desires). Both *Vincent* and *Lightfoot* translate it, "to pay court to," ostensibly, as a lover pays court to his lady. The Judaizers were zealously paying court to the Galatians. Paul adds, "but not well." *Well* is from *kalos*. The Judaizers were paying court to the Galatians, but not in an honorable way. What was dishonorable about their paying court to the Galatians is told us in the words of Paul, "Yea, they would exclude you, that ye might affect them."

The word *exclude* is from *ekkleio* which means "to shut out." That from which the Judaizers wished to shut out the Galatians, is not stated in so many words. The context suggests that the Judaizers were attempting to shut the Galatians out, either from the benefits of the gospel of grace, or from fellowship with Paul and his companions who maintained that the Gentiles are accepted by God on the basis of faith without works. In either case, the result would be that the Galatians would turn to the Judaizers for guidance and fellowship, and the latter would be in a position where the Galatians would be paying court to them. However, it would be more natural to speak of shutting out the Galatians from the benefits of the gospel, since the verb *ekkleio* favors that, and because a verb meaning "to alienate or cause separation from" would be more natural if Paul meant that the Judaizers were attempting to separate the Galatians from Paul. Thus, the idea is that the Judaizers were zealously paying court to the Galatians, attempting to shut them out from the benefits of the gospel in order that they (the Galatians) might have to pay court to the Judaizers, since they would have no refuge for their souls elsewhere.

Translation. *They are zealously paying you court, but not honestly, desiring to isolate you in order that you might be paying court to them.*

Verses eighteen and nineteen. Paul says, "But it is good to be zealously courted at all times in a good thing, and not only when I am present with you." He refers here probably to his own persistent courting of the Galatians. He says that the fact that someone else pays them court, and that they court the favor of others, is not wrong in itself. He says that he himself is not insensible to such attachments. He remembers how warm were

GREEK NEW TESTAMENT

the feelings of the Galatians toward him when he was with them, and he yearns for their continued cordiality towards himself. Paul courted the Galatians, not to attach them to himself, but that he might join them to the Lord Jesus. He was glad that they should be courted at all times, even by others in his absence, if it is done in a right spirit and in connection with the truth of the gospel.

Translation. *But it is good to be zealously courted in a good thing at all times, and not only when I am present with you, my little children, of whom I travail in birth again until Christ be formed in you.*

The Greek text shows that the words "my little children," are not in the vocative case, introducing a fresh appeal, but an accusative in apposition with the pronoun *you* of verse 18. This is the language of deep affection and emotion, in which Paul asserts his rights to hold the love of the Galatians. He speaks of them as his children (*tekna, born ones*). He is for the second time distressed for his Galatian converts with the same anguish that he experienced in his efforts at their conversion. The metaphor speaking of a Christian winning converts to the Lord Jesus, as those who give birth to spiritual children, is found in I Corinthians 4:15 and Philemon 10. It was a Jewish saying, "If one teaches the son of his neighbor the law, the Scripture reckons this the same as though he had begotten him."

The word *formed* is from *morphoo* which refers to the act of giving outward expression of one's inner nature. We use the English word *form* in that way sometimes. For instance, "I went to the tennis match yesterday. The winning player's form was excellent." We mean by that, that the outward expression which he gave of his inward ability to play tennis, was excellent.

In our Galatian verse, Paul refers to the outward expression of the Lord Jesus in the lives of the Galatian Christians. These to whom Paul was writing, were truly saved. The Lord Jesus was resident in their hearts. But there was little of His beauty in their lives. The word *again* tells us that at one time He was clearly and abundantly evident in their experience. But now

He ceased to be seen in the lives of the Galatian Christians. The reason is found in the fact that the Judaizers in placing the Galatian Christians under law, had caused them to substitute self effort in an attempt to obey a newly imposed law, for their previous dependence upon the Holy Spirit for the production of a Christ-like life in and through them. The passive voice of the verb "be formed," tells us that the Lord Jesus dwells in the heart of a Christian in a passive way, and thus does not express Himself through the Christian. He has given that ministry over to the Holy Spirit. He said, referring to the Spirit, "That One shall glorify Me" (John 16:14). The Holy Spirit was not being recognized and depended upon by the Galatians. Consequently He was not able to minister the Lord Jesus to and through the Galatians in a full measure. What havoc the Judaizers were working in the Galatian churches.[22]

Translation. *But it is good to be zealously courted in a good thing at all times, and not only when I am present with you, my born ones, concerning whom I am again striving with intense effort and anguish until Christ be outwardly expressed in you.*

Verse twenty. Paul, concerned about the unhappy situation in the Galatian churches (4:11), moved by his deep love for the Galatian believers (4:19), and perplexed as to how he could help them in this present crisis (4:20), expresses the wish that he might be with them personally. He desired to be present in order that he could "change his voice." These last words could mean either or both of two things, each in perfect harmony with the context.

First, they could mean that the apostle regretted the severity of his language on the occasion of his second visit to the Galatian churches at which time he had warned them against the Judaizers, and that he desired to be with them personally in order that he might talk to them in a more tender and affectionate manner, however, still telling them the truth. For a similar instance in which he for a time regretted the stern tone he used see II Corinthians 7:8.

---

22. *Riches,* pp. 74-78.

Second, the words "to change my voice," were regularly used of the act of changing to some other means of expression. Paul longs to go to them and speak personally rather than send a message through the medium of writing. *Robertson* says in connection with this passage, "Paul could put his heart into his voice. The pen stands between them. He knew the power of his voice on their hearts."[23] But the apostle found it impossible to go to them at that time, and thus in the providence of God, the Church has the letter to the Galatians, and has found it a tower of strength and a bulwark against the heresy which teaches that salvation is appropriated by faith plus works.

Both of these interpretations could be true, and could be included in what Paul meant by these words. He desired to be with the Galatians personally so that he might speak to them face to face instead of writing a letter, and in speaking to them, change his tone from one of severity to one of gentleness.

The word *now* is not from *nun* but from *arti,* which latter word more sharply defines and particularizes the point of time referred to in the context. One could translate it by the words "at this very moment." The words "stand in doubt" are from *aporeo.* The word finds its base in *poros,* "a transit, a ford, a way, revenue, resource," and has the Greek letter *alpha* prefixed which negates the meaning of the word, and thus it comes to mean, "to be without a way or path, not to know which way to turn, to be without resources, to be in straits, to be in perplexity." That was Paul's position with regard to his Galatian converts. The verb is in the middle voice, which fact speaks of the inward distress of a mind tossed to and fro by conflicting doubts and fears. The Greek has it, "I am perplexed in you." Paul's perplexity is conceived as being in the Galatians. He says in effect, "I am puzzled how to deal with you, how to find an entrance into your hearts."

Translation. *Moreover, I was wishing that I were present with you at this very moment, and could thus change my tone, because I am perplexed about you.*

---

23. *Word Pictures in the New Testament.*

VIII. *The history of Hagar and Sarah illustrates the present status of law and grace. As the son of the bondwoman gave place to the son of the freewoman, so law has given place to grace (4:21-31).*

Verse twenty one. The words "ye that desire to be under the law," imply that the Galatians had not adopted, but were on the point of adopting the law. The idea is, "ye who are bent on being under law." The article is absent before *law* in the Greek text. The word *law* here refers to law as a principle of life, not only to the Mosaic law. The apostle asks the Galatians who are bent on being under law, "Are ye not hearing the law?" This is a remonstrance to these Galatians who are bent on upholding the authority of the law, but who are not heeding the full significance of that law.

Translation. *Tell me, ye that are bent upon being under law, are ye not hearing the law?*

Verse twenty two. The word *for* connects the contents of verse 21 with those of 22. The idea is, "Your desire to be under law is not in harmony with Scripture, and here is the scripture." The word *bondmaid* is the translation of *paidiske*, a term frequently used in the LXX of a female slave.

Translation. *For it stands written, Abraham had two sons, one from the maidservant and one from the freewoman.*

Verse twenty three. Ishmael, born of the bondwoman, was born after the flesh, that is, by natural generation in the ordinary course of nature. But Isaac, born of the freewoman, was born according to promise, through the miraculous interposition of God, when the parents were too old to have children. The words "was born," are in the perfect tense in preference to the usual aorist, because Paul was not thinking simply of the historic fact of the two births, but of the existing results. Ishmael's descendants do not belong to the covenant people, Israel. Isaac's descendants are those that have the promises. In verse 22, Ishmael and Isaac are coupled together as the sons of one father. Here they are contrasted in that they each had a different mother.

Translation. *But on the one hand, the son of the maidservant was one born in the ordinary course of nature. On the other hand, the son of the freewoman was one born through the promise.*

Verse twenty four. Paul says that the story of Hagar and Ishmael and Sarah and Isaac, is an allegory. This does not mean that he is casting doubt upon the historical trustworthiness of the patriarchal narrative in Genesis. An allegory is a statement of facts which is to be understood literally, and yet requires or justly admits a moral or a figurative interpretation. Paul, while using the story as an illustration, does so in order to prove his argument to the effect that the law is superseded by grace. Then he speaks of the covenant of law that was given at Mt. Sinai. This is allegorically identified with Hagar. This covenant places its children in a condition of bondage.

Translation. *Which class of things is allegorical. For these are two covenants, one from Mount Sinai, begetting bondage, which is as to its nature classed as Hagar.*

Verse twenty five. The exact meaning of the statement, "For this Hagar is Mount Sinai," is in debate among commentators. A possible interpretation is as follows: The word *Hagar* in this verse is not used of the woman Hagar, but is another designation of Mount Sinai. The name *Hagar* resembles the Arabic name of Sinai. The Arabians are called sons of Hagar.

This Hagar or Sinai corresponds, Paul says, to the then existent city of Jerusalem, the center of the apostate observance of Judaism. Just as Hagar, a slave, bore children that by birth became slaves, so the followers of legalistic Judaism are in bondage to law.

Translation. *Now this Hagar is Mount Sinai in Arabia, and corresponds to the Jerusalem which now is, for she is in bondage with her children.*

Verse twenty six. The phrase "Jerusalem which is above," was familiar to the rabbinical teachers who thought of the heavenly Jerusalem as the archtype of the earthly. The heavenly Jerusalem which is free, therefore represents Sarah; and finally, grace, and the faith way of salvation, for it is contrasted to the earthly Jerusalem which represents legalistic Judaism.

Translation. *But the Jerusalem which is above is free, which is our Mother.*

Verse twenty seven. This verse is a quotation from Isaiah 54:1, and follows the LXX. The words are applied to the unfruitful Sarah who answers to the heavenly Jerusalem.

Translation. *For it stands written, Rejoice, barren (woman) who does not bear. Break forth and cry, you who do not travail, because more are the children of the desolate than of the one who has an husband.*

Verse twenty eight. The best texts have *ye* instead of *we*. Paul is assuring the Galatian Christians that they are not like Ishmael the son of the slave woman, but like Isaac who was born according to the promise, not in the usual course of nature but miraculously. So they are born of the Holy Spirit, and have their standing before God, not on the basis of physical descent from Abraham, but upon the promise made to Abraham which applies to all who have like faith to him.

Translation. *And, as for you, brethren, after the manner of Isaac are ye children of promise.*

Verse twenty nine. The reference is to Ishmael who persecuted Isaac (Gen. 21:9). So the Judaizers were persecuting Paul and all those who would not forsake grace for law.

Translation. *But just as then he who was born according to the flesh was constantly persecuting him who was born according to the Spirit, so also now.*

Verse thirty. Paul, in interpreting the allegory, says that the rejection of Ishmael points to a rejection of the children of Abraham after the flesh in favor of those who become children of Abraham by faith. *Lightfoot* has the following to say about these words of the apostle Paul. "The law and the gospel cannot coexist. The law must disappear before the gospel. It is scarcely possible to estimate the strength of conviction and depth of prophetic insight which this declaration implies. The apostle thus confidently sounds the death-knell of Judaism at a time when one half of Christendom clung to the Mosaic law with a jealous affection little short of frenzy, and while the Judaic party seemed to be growing in influence, and was strong enough even in the Gentile churches of his own founding to undermine his influence and endanger his life. The truth which to us appears a truism, must then have been regarded as a paradox."

Translation. *But what does the Scripture say? Throw out the maidservant and her son. For the son of the maidservant shall by no means inherit with the son of the freewoman.*

Verse thirty one. This verse brings to a climax the argument that believers are not a community or nation in bondage to legal statutes, but members of the community of believers whose relation to God is that of sons, and who do not have the spirit of bondage but the Spirit of sonship. It also serves as the basis upon which Paul builds the practical instruction which follows in chapters five and six.

Translation. *Therefore, brethren, we are children not of a maidservant, but of the freewoman.*

PRACTICAL

In 1:11-2:21, Paul shows that he was divinely commissioned as an apostle and as such was not answerable to the Twelve in Jerusalem. In chapters 3 and 4, he defends his doctrine of justification by faith alone, against the Judaizers who added works to faith as the necessary conditions for salvation. In 5:1-6:10, the inspired apostle presents practical teaching and exhortation designed to correct the havoc which the teaching of the Judaizers was causing in the personal lives of the Galatian Christians. In 4:19 Paul expresses the wish that the Lord Jesus might again be outwardly expressed in their lives. The Galatians had lost His beauty which before the coming of the Judaizers had been so prominent in their experience. The Lord Jesus was not being expressed in their lives as heretofore. This was the direct result of the Judaizer's legalistic teachings. The Galatian Christians, instead of depending upon the indwelling Spirit to produce in their lives the beauty of the Lord Jesus, now were depending upon self-effort in an attempt to obey law. Accordingly, Paul's practical teaching emphasizes the ministry of the Spirit, and the Galatians are exhorted to put themselves again under His control.

I. *Paul exhorts the Galatians to hold fast to the freedom from law which the Lord Jesus had procured for them by the blood of His Cross, and not to become entangled again in a legalistic system* (5:1-12).

Verse one. We can best approach the study of this verse by offering the translation at the start. *For this aforementioned freedom, Christ set us free. Keep on standing firm therefore, and stop being held again by a yoke of bondage.* The word *free* of 4:31 is the translation of the same Greek word rendered *liberty* in this verse. The word is dative of advantage. The teaching is that Christ died on the Cross to give us the advantage of having this liberty or freedom. This liberty consists of the Christian's freedom from the law. Under the law, the person has no more liberty than a child in its minority under a guardian. The child has no freedom of action nor right of self-determination. He must move within a set of rules prescribed by his guardian. He is not old enough to act alone. He must always act under the restrictions of his guardian. So is it with the person under the law. Here were these Galatian Christians, free from the law, having been placed in the family of God as adult sons, indwelt by the Holy Spirit who would enable them to act out in their experience that maturity of Christian life in which they were placed, now putting on the straight-jacket of the law, cramping their experience, stultifying their actions, depriving themselves of the power of the Holy Spirit. They were like adults putting themselves under rules made for children.

The liberty spoken of here does not refer to the kind of life a person lives, neither does it have reference to his words and actions, but it has to do with the method by which he lives that life. The Judaizers lived their lives by dependence upon self effort in an attempt to obey the law. The Galatian Christians had been living their's in dependence upon the indwelling Holy

Spirit. Their hearts had been occupied with the Lord Jesus, the details of their lives being guided by the ethics that emerged from the teaching of the apostles, both doctrinal and practical. Now, in swinging over to law, they were losing that freedom of action and that flexibility of self-determination which one exercises in the doing of what is right, when one does right, not because the law forbids the wrong and commands the right, but because it is right, because it pleases the Lord Jesus, and because of love for Him. Paul exhorts them to keep on standing fast in that freedom from law.

The word *entangled* is from *enecho*, which means "to be held within, to be ensnared." It is used of those who are held in a physical (net or the like) or ethical (law, dogma, emotion) restriction upon their liberty, so that they are unable to free themselves. The Galatian Christians, having escaped from the slavery of heathenism, were in danger of becoming entangled in the meshes of legalistic Judaism. Paul in 4:1-7 had already told them of the fact that grace had placed them as adult sons in the family of God, and in 4:8-10 had asked them how it was that they were turning back to such an elementary method of living their lives. Now, in 5:1 he enforces his exhortation and launches out into a discussion of the Spirit-filled life.[24]

Translation. *For this aforementioned freedom Christ set you free. Keep on standing firm therefore, and stop being held in again by a yoke of bondage.*

Verse two. The words "if ye be circumcised," present an hypothetical case. The Galatians had not yet submitted to that rite, but were on the verge of doing so. The words "Christ shall profit you nothing," must be interpreted in their context. Paul is not speaking here of their standing in grace as justified believers. He is speaking of the method of living a Christian life and of growth in that life. Thus, if the Galatians submit to circumcision, they are putting themselves under law, and are depriving themselves of the ministry of the Holy Spirit which Christ made possible through His death and resurrection, and which

---

24. For a fresh study of the ministry of the Spirit based on the Greek text, to supplement the teaching in Galatians, see the author's book, *Untranslatable Riches*.

ministry was not provided for under law. In the Old Testament dispensation, the Spirit came upon or in believers in order that they might perform a certain service for God, and then left them when that service was accomplished. He did not indwell them for purposes of sanctification. The great apostle had taught the Galatians that God's grace guaranteed their everlasting retention of salvation, and so they understood that he was speaking of their Christian experience, not their Christian standing.

Translation. *Behold, I, Paul, am saying to you that if you go on (persist in) being circumcised, Christ will be advantageous to you in not even one thing.*

Verse three. This verse continues the argument of verse 2. Not only would the Galatians lose the aid of the Holy Spirit in the living of their Christian lives, but they would be assuming the burden of the entire legalistic system. Paul warns them that the acceptance of circumcision would be in principle the acceptance of the whole of that system. The fact that Paul points this out to the Galatians, implies that the Judaizers had not done so. They were now asking the Galatian Christians to accept circumcision as a rite by which they would become sons of Abraham and thus participants in the blessings of the Abrahamic Covenant. The Judaizers had already persuaded them to adopt the Jewish cycle of feasts.

The words "I testify," are from *marturomai* which without an object accusative as it is here, signifies, not "to call to witness" but "to affirm, to protest." It is a strong asseveration, not merely a simple testimony. The word *again* refers to a like statement made to the Galatians, probably on the occasion referred to in 4:16 and 1:9. The words "every man who is circumcised," do not refer to the fact that the Galatians had accepted circumcision. That would call for the perfect tense. The present is used here. The idea is "everyone who receives circumcision." The warning is addressed, not to the man who has been circumcised, but to the one contemplating doing so.

The word *debtor* is from *opheiletes,* which refers to one who is under obligation, one who is bound to do a certain thing, here in effect, to one who binds himself to something. The obligation is as the context shows, one which the Christian ought not to assume. The believer is free from the law in three respects. *First,* he is free from the condemnation it imposes upon the one who would disobey it. *Second,* he is free from the law as a means of justification. *Third,* he is free from the obligation to render obedience to its statutes. The believer in this Age of Grace is obligated to obey either all of the law or none of it. If he feels that he is obligated to obey parts of it which he chooses, that, for instance, obligates him to keep the Sabbath, the seventh day, instead of the first day of the week, the Lord's Day. By what rule can one isolate certain parts of the Old Testament law as binding upon Christians and disregard other parts as purely Jewish in their application? The Galatians were not obligated to obey any of the law. Submission of the Galatians to the rite of circumcision, makes them a party to the covenant of the law, and the law requires from everyone thus committed, a full and perfect obedience. *The ethics of the Pauline epistles and the ministry of the Holy Spirit, take the place of and are an advance upon the Mosaic economy of regeneration and the objective written law. Whatever is of value for the Church in the legal enactments of the Mosaic code, is found in the hortatory passages of the New Testament epistles.* That is not to say, however, that the great principles of conduct underlying the statutes of the Mosaic law, are to be ignored. The Old Testament, even though superseded by the New which is specially designed for the Church, yet has great value to the latter. Still it must be used with the following two guiding principles in mind; *first,* it is specially adapted to the needs of the nation Israel and for the time before the Cross, and *second,* its legal enactments where they deal with general principles of conduct that are universal and eternal in their application, must never be treated as legally binding upon the believer but only as ethics to guide his conduct.

Translation. *And I solemnly affirm again to every man who receives circumcision, that he is under obligation to do the whole law.*

Verse four. The words "Christ is become of no effect unto you," must be understood in their context to refer, not to their justification but to their spiritual lives as Christians. The apostle is not here speaking of their standing but of their experience. The words "become of no effect," are from *katergeo* which means "to make ineffectual," and which used with the word *apo* (from) as it is here, means "to be without effect from, to be unaffected by, to be without effective relation to." The word is applied to any destruction of growth or life, physical or spiritual. Joined with *apo* (from), it speaks of the loss of some essential element of life by the severance of previous intimate relations. The subject of the verb here is the Galatian Christians. One could translate "You have become unaffected by Christ," or, "You have become without effective relation to Christ." The idea is that the Galatian Christians, by putting themselves under law, have put themselves in a place where they have ceased to be in that relation to Christ where they could derive the spiritual benefits from Him which would enable them to live a life pleasing to Him, namely, through the ministry of the Holy Spirit. Thus, Christ has no more effect upon them in the living of their Christian lives.

In depriving themselves of the ministry of the Holy Spirit in the living of a Christian life, they have fallen from grace. The words "fallen from" are from *ekpipto* which means "to fail of, to lose one's hold of." The Galatian Christians had lost their hold upon the grace for daily living which heretofore had been ministered to them by the Holy Spirit. God's grace manifests itself in three ways, in justification, sanctification, and glorification. The context rules. All through chapter five, Paul is talking about the Holy Spirit's ministry to the believer. Therefore *grace* here must be interpreted as the daily grace for living of which the Galatian Christians were depriving themselves.

But because they had lost their hold upon sanctifying grace, does not mean that God's grace had lost its hold upon them in the sphere of justification. Because they had refused to accept God's grace in sanctification is no reason why God should withdraw His grace for justification. They had received the latter when they accepted the Lord Jesus. That transaction was closed and permanent at the moment they believed. Justification is a judicial act of God done once for all. Sanctification is a process which goes on all through the Christian's life. *Just because the process of sanctification is temporarily retarded in a believer's life, does not say that his justification is taken away. If that were the case, then the retention of salvation would depend upon the believer's works, and then salvation would not depend upon grace anymore. And we find ourselves in the camp of the Judaizers, ancient and modern.*

Translation. *You are without effect from Christ, such of you as in the sphere of the law are seeking your justification. You have lost your hold upon grace.*

Verse five. The righteousness spoken of here is not justifying righteousness, and for three reasons. *First,* it is righteousness which finds its source in the operation of the Holy Spirit. Justifying righteousness is a purely legal matter and has to do with a believer's standing before God. The Holy Spirit has nothing to do with that. That is a matter between God the Father and God the Son. The Father justifies a believing sinner on the basis of the work of the Son on the Cross. *Second,* the context is dealing with the Christian's experience, not his standing, with the method of living a Christian life, not the relation of that person to the laws of God. *Third,* love as a fruit of the Holy Spirit in the life of the Christian, is spoken of in verse 6, which verse is bound up with verse 5. This again shows that the grace spoken of in verse 5 is sanctifying grace, of which latter the Galatian saints were depriving themselves by their act of depending upon self effort in an attempt to obey law.

Paul says that it is through the agency of the Spirit that we can hope for the presence of an experimental righteousness in the life, not by self effort. The word *we* is emphatic. It is, "as for us, we (Christians) through the Spirit wait for the hope of righteousness by faith," not as the Judaizers who attempted to live a righteous life by self effort rather than by dependence upon the Holy Spirit. The phrase "the hope of righteousness," is a construction of the Greek text called an objective genitive. It can be translated "the hoped-for righteousness." It is that righteousness which is the object of hope. The words "by faith," are to be construed with "wait." We wait for this hoped-for righteousness by faith. The word *wait* is from a*podechomai*. The same word is used in Philippians 3:20, and there translated *look*. The word speaks of an attitude of intense yearning and an eager waiting for something. Here it refers to the believer's intense desire for and eager expectation of a practical righteousness which will be constantly produced in his life by the Holy Spirit as he yields himself to Him.

Translation. *For, as for us, through the agency of the Spirit, on the ground of faith, a hoped-for righteousness we are eagerly awaiting.*

Verse six. The word *availeth* is the translation of *ischuo* which which means "to have power, to exert or wield power." Thus, in the case of the one who is joined to Christ Jesus in that life-giving union which was effected through the act of the Holy Spirit baptizing the believing sinner into the Lord Jesus (Romans 6:3, 4), the fact that he is circumcised or is not circumcised, has no power for anything in his life. The thing that is of power to effect a transformation in the life is faith, the faith of the justified person which issues in love in his life, a love produced by the Holy Spirit.

Translation. *For in Christ Jesus, neither circumcision is of any power nor uncircumcision, but faith coming to effective expression through love.*

Verse seven. The words "did run" are in the imperfect tense, referring to a continuous action going on in past time. Here, as in 4:12, Paul breaks off his argument to make an appeal to his readers on the basis of their past experience. He uses the figure of a Greek runner. "You were running well." The word *well* is from *kalos*, suggesting the translation, "You were conducting yourselves bravely, honorably, becomingly." The word *hinder* is from *enkopto* which means "to cut in, to make an incision, to hinder." Inasmuch as Paul is using the figure of a race, this word suggests a breaking into the race course, a cutting in on a runner by another runner, thus slowing up his progress. The Galatian Christians were running the Christian race well, but the Judaizers cut in on them and now were slowing up their progress in their growth in the Christian life. They had deprived the Galatians of the ministry of the Holy Spirit, and the latter had been thrown back upon self effort in an attempt to obey a set of legal restrictions, with the result that their lives had lost the fragrance of the Lord Jesus and the enabling power for service which the Spirit formerly gave them. The question Paul asks is rhetorical, not for information. The great apostle knew well enough who had slowed up the Christian growth of the Galatians.

Translation. *You were running well. Who cut in on you and thus hindered you from obeying the truth?*

Verse eight. The word *persuasion* is from *peismone,* the verb of the same root being *peitho,* which latter means "to persuade," that is, "to induce one by words to believe." The word is used here in an active sense. It refers to the act of the Judaizers inducing the Galatians to believe their preaching. This activity of the Judaizers, Paul says, does not come from the One who called them into salvation, namely, God. This negative statement indicates that the influence which was turning them away from grace was hostile to God. He definitely expresses this in the next verse where he speaks of the teachings of the Judaizers as leaven, the term *leaven* always referring in Scripture to evil, here to false doctrine. The definite article before the word *persuasion* in the Greek text, identifies the persuasion as that which cut into the Galatian's progress in the Christian life mentioned in verse 7, namely, the teachings of the Judaizers. God who called them, called them to freedom in Christ, not to the enslaving tenets of the Judaizers.

Translation. *This persuasion is not from the One who calls you.*

Verse nine. Leaven is always a symbol of evil in the Bible. The Jews before the days of unleavened bread, would remove every particle of leaven from their homes. Leaven, which operates on the principle of fermentation, is an apt symbol of moral and spiritual corruption. A very small lump readily permeates the entire bread dough. Our Lord used it as a symbol of the false doctrines of the scribes and Pharisees (Matt. 16:6-12). In I Corinthians 5:6, Paul uses the symbol, of the immoral conduct of a few in the church which was endangering the life of the entire church, and which unrebuked, would spread throughout that local assembly. The symbol appears to have had a wide usage as a proverbial saying referring to the tendency of an influence, even though small, to spread so as to control the entire situation or surroundings. The insidious work of these Judaizers was slowly permeating the religious life of the Galatian churches. The verb is in the present tense, indicating that the process of doctrinal fermentation was going on, but that it had not yet corrupted the entire church structure. It had made but a little progress. Paul was more alarmed over its insidious nature than over the extent to which it had permeated the churches.

Translation. *A little leaven is leavening the whole lump.*

Verse ten. Paul now turns with decided abruptness from the discouraging picture of verse 9 to one of encouragement. The personal pronoun *ego* (*I*) appears in the Greek text. It emphasizes the personal character of Paul's confidence in them. It is, "I, at least, whatever others may think." The word *confidence* is from *peitho*, "to persuade," and in the perfect tense. Paul had come to a settled persuasion or conviction regarding them. The words "through the Lord," speak of the Lord Jesus, not primarily as the object of trust, but as the One who is the basis or ground of Paul's confidence. The words "none otherwise," tell us that Paul expected the Galatians to take no other view of the source of the Judaizer's message than he took, namely, that it did not come from God but from an evil source, and that the leaven of the Judaizers was false doctrine. The words "be minded," are from *phroneo* which denotes a general disposition of the mind rather than a specific act of thought directed at a given point.

The word *troubleth* is from *tarasso* which is used of the act of disturbing the faith of someone. The word *bear* is from *bastazo* which speaks of a grievous burden. The judgment of God would be the grievous burden which anyone would have to bear who would disturb the faith of the Galatian Christians.

Translation. As for myself, I have come to a settled confidence in the Lord with respect to you, namely, that you will take no other view than this. But the one who troubles you shall bear his judgment, whoever he is.

Verse eleven. The Judaizers said that Paul was still preaching circumcision when it suited his purpose. Paul answers this charge by calling the attention of the Galatians to the fact that he was still being persecuted, implying that it was for his anti-legalism. The first *yet* is from *eti,* which word speaks of a thing that went on formerly, whereas now a different state of things exists. The implication is clear that Paul at one time preached the necessity of circumcision as a means of acceptance with God. There is no evidence to prove that he included that in his preaching after he was saved. It is clear that he made a clean break with legalism as a method of salvation before he commenced his ministry. The Book of Acts records the fact that he was continually being persecuted by the Jews because of his break with the Mosaic economy. It was as a Pharisee that he had preached circumcision. The word *if* is from *ei.* It is a contrary-to-fact condition. Paul denies that he is preaching circumcision. The first *yet* is temporal, and one could translate by the word *still.* The second *yet* denotes logical opposition. The idea is, "If I am still preaching circumcision, why am I in spite of that fact being persecuted?"

The persecution of Paul had its basis in the fact that the Cross was an offense to the Jew. What made the Cross an offense to the Jew? Paul tells us in the words, "If I yet preach circumcision, then is the offense of the cross ceased." That is, if circumcision be preached as one of the prerequisites of salvation, then the Cross of Christ would cease to be an offense. Thus, the offensiveness of the Cross to the Jew lay in the teaching that believers in the Lord Jesus are free from the Mosaic law. That was the very point at issue when the Sanhedrin was trying Stephen. The charge was not that he was worshipping the Crucified One. It was that he was speaking blasphemous words against the Jewish

Temple and the law of Moses (Acts 6:13, 14). Chrysostom commenting on this same thing said, "For even the cross which was a stumbling block to the Jews, was not so much so as the failure to require obedience to ancestral laws. For when they attacked Stephen they said not that he was worshipping the Crucified, but that he was speaking against the law and the holy place." Saul, the Pharisee, persecuted the Church for the same reason (1:13, 14). The Cross was offensive to the Jew therefore because it set aside the entire Mosaic economy, and because it offered salvation by grace through faith alone without the added factor of works performed by the sinner in an effort to merit the salvation offered. All of which goes to show that the Jew of the first century had an erroneous conception of the law of Moses, for that system never taught that a sinner was accepted by God on the basis of good works.

The word *ceased* is from *katergeo* which means "to render idle or inoperative, put to an end, abolish." The word *offense* is from *skandalon* which means, "a stumbling block."

Translation. *And I, brethren, if I am still preaching circumcision, why am I in spite of this fact being persecuted? Then the stumbling-block of the Cross has been done away with.*

Verse twelve. The words *cut off* are from *apokopto*. The word refers to bodily mutilation. Paul expresses the wish that the Judaizers would not stop with circumcision, but would go on to emasculation. The town of Pessinus was the home of the worship of Cybele in honor of whom bodily mutilation was practiced. The priests of Cybele castrated themselves. This was a recognized form of heathen self-devotion to the god and would not be shunned in ordinary conversation. This explains the freedom with which Paul speaks of it to his Galatian converts. In Philippians 3:2, the apostle speaks of the Judaizers as the concision, that is, those who mutilate themselves. *Vincent* expresses his conception of Paul's words as follows: "These people are disturbing you by insisting on circumcision. I would that they would make thorough work of it in their own case, and instead of merely amputating the foreskin, would castrate themselves as heathen priests do. Perhaps this would be even more powerful help to salvation." He says that this is perhaps the severest expression in Paul's epistles. The great danger in which Christianity was placed by the Judaizers, made such a severe statement necessary. The man who could beseech his converts with the meekness and gentleness of Christ, could also deal in a most severe way when the occasion for such treatment presented itself. The whole expression shows that circumcision had become for Paul a purely physical act without religious significance, and, performed for such a purpose as that for which the Judaizers used it, it became a bodily mutilation not different in character to the mutilations of the heathen religions. Thus, by glorying in the flesh, the Galatians would be returning to the bondage of their former heathenism.

The word *trouble* is from *anastatoo* which means "to upset or overthrow." It is used of driving one out of his home, of ruining a city. The word forcibly expresses the revolutionary character of the agitation with which the Judaizers were upsetting the peace and the order of the Galatian churches.

The words *I would* are from *opheilo* which when coupled with the future tense as it is here, does not express a wish, but speaks of that which ought to be the logical outcome of the present. The statement predicts in a bitter and ironic fashion what this superstitious worship of circumcision must lead to where men exalt an ordinance of the flesh above the necessity of faith in Christ, namely, to self-mutilation as was the practice of the heathen world of that time.

Translation. *I would that they who are upsetting you, would even have themselves mutilated.*

II. *You have been liberated from the law by the blood of Christ. But do not think that this freedom gives you the liberty to sin. The reason why you have been liberated from such an elementary method of controlling the conduct of an individual, is that you might be free to live your life on a new principle, namely, under the control of the Holy Spirit* (5:13-26).

1. *He warns them not to use their freedom from the law as a pretext for sinning, thus turning liberty into license. He exhorts them instead, to govern their lives by the motivating impulse of a Spirit-produced divine love (5:13-15).*

Verse thirteen. The sentence, "For, brethren, ye have been called unto liberty," is transitional, reaching back to all that has preceded it, summing up the whole preceding argument for Christian liberty, and looking ahead to what follows in that it introduces a wholly new aspect of the matter of Christian liberty, the danger of abusing it. To those who have been accustomed to regard law as the only controlling factor that stands in the way of self-indulgence and a free rein in sin, and to those who have not been accustomed to a high standard of ethics, the teaching of Christian liberty might easily mean that there is nothing to stand in the way of the unrestrained indulgence of one's own impulses. Paul often during his ministry, had his hearers react in this way to his teaching of grace. The questions in Romans 6:1 and 6:15, *Shall we continue in sin, that grace may abound?* and, *Shall we sin because we are not under law but under grace?* were asked by someone who did not understand grace. Paul answers these questions in Romans 6, by showing that the control of the sinful nature over the individual is broken the moment he believes, and the divine nature is imparted, and therefore he hates sin and loves the right, and has both the desire and power to keep from sinning and to do God's will.[25] In Galatians he shows that the believer has come out from under whatever control divine law had over him, and in salvation has been placed under a superior control, that of the indwelling Holy Spirit who exercises a stricter supervision over the believer than law ever did over the unbeliever, whose restraining power is far more effective than the law's restraining power ever was, and who gives the believer both the desire and power to refuse the wrong and choose the right, a thing which law never was able to do. The believer therefore has passed out of one control into

---

25. *Treasures*, pp. 79-106.

another, from the control of a mere system of legal enactments into the control of a Person, God the Holy Spirit. When God abrogated the law at the Cross, He knew what He was doing. He did not leave the world without a restraining hand. He ran this world for 2500 years before the Mosaic law was enacted. He can run it again without the Mosaic law. He does not need the help of legalistic teachers and preachers in the Church who think they are helping Him control this world by imposing law on grace. Indeed, it is the general ignorance and lack of recognition of the ministry of the Holy Spirit that is responsible for the tendency in the Church of adding law to grace. There is a recognition of the fact that the flesh is still with the Christian even though its power over him is broken, and consequently a feeling that even the child of God still needs a restraint put upon him. And this is as it should be. But the mistake that is made so often is that the Mosaic law is substituted for the restraint of the Holy Spirit, and with disastrous results. Not only does the law not restrain evil, but on the other hand it brings out evil in the life because the fallen nature rebels against it (Rom. 7:7-13), and the latter is thus incited to evil. The Holy Spirit strove with men before the Mosaic law was given. He still continues to do so. And what is more, He indwells the Church and has the cooperation of the Christian in His work of restraining evil. He will restrain evil through the Church until He goes to Heaven as He takes the Church with Him (II Thess. 2:7). He will still be restraining evil during the Great Tribulation, since He is omnipresent. No preacher ever enables the Christians to whom he ministers, to live a better Christian life by putting them under the Ten Words from Sinai and by letting them smell the brimstone of the Lake of Fire. A policeman on the street corner is a far more efficient deterrent of law-breaking than any number of city ordinances placarded for public notice. To acquaint the saint with the ministry of the indwelling Holy Spirit, is far more productive of victory over sin than the imposition of the law. The controlling ministry of the Holy Spirit is the secret of holy living. And that is Paul's thesis here.

The word *occasion* is from *aphorme*. It is a military term speaking of a base of operations. In our Galatian passage it means "the cause, occasion, or pretext" of a thing. Paul exhorts the Galatians not to make their liberty from the law a base of operations from which to serve sin. Their liberty was not to be used as a spring-board from which to take off with the intention of sinning.

The antidote against using their liberty from the law as a pretext for sinning, is found in the exhortation, "By love serve one another." The Greek word for *love* here is *agape*, which refers, not to human affection but to divine love, the love produced in the heart of the yielded believer by the Holy Spirit, and the love with which that believer should love his fellow-believers. This love is a love whose chief essence is self-sacrifice for the benefit of the one who is loved. Such a love means death to self, and that means defeat for sin, since the essence of sin is self-will and self-gratification. The word *serve* is from *douloo* which means "to render service to, to do that which is for the advantage of someone else." It is the word Paul used when he spoke of the slavery that is imposed by the law upon the one who is under law. The Galatian Christians were rescued from the slavery which legalism imposed, and brought into a new servitude, that of a loving, glad, and willing service to God and man which annihilates self and subordinates all selfish desires to love. This is the secret of victory over the totally depraved nature whose power over the believer was broken when God saved him, when that nature attempts to induce the Christian to use his liberty as a pretext to sin.

Translation. *For, as for you, upon the basis of freedom you were called, brethren. Only do not turn your liberty into a base of operations for the flesh, but through love keep on constantly serving one another.*

Verse fourteen. The apostle has up to this point bent all his efforts at dissuading the Galatians from coming under bondage to law again. Now he exhorts them to love one another. If they do this he says, they will fulfill the law. But how are we to understand this? In Romans 8:4 Paul speaks of the fact that **the righteousness of the law is fulfilled in the Christian by the Holy Spirit.** There is therefore a sense in which the word *law* is used other than in the legalistic sense in which Paul has used it throughout this letter so far. It is that sense in which it is conceived of as divine law consisting of ethical principals and standards that inhere in the being of God, and represent those things that go to make up right conduct on the part of man.

Paul's statement becomes intelligible and consistent when we recognize the following points; *first,* that believers through their new relation to the Lord Jesus, are released from the whole law as statutes, and from the obligation to obey its statutes, *second,* that all which God's law as an expression of His will requires, is included in love, and *third,* when the believer acts on the principle of love, he is fulfilling in his actions toward God, his fellowman, and himself, all that the Mosaic law would require of him in his position in life were that law in force. The statutes of the law, the believer will incidently obey so far as love itself requires such a course of action of him, and in no case will he obey them as statutes. Thus, the individual is released from one law consisting of a set of ethical principles to which was attached blessing for obedience and punishment in the case of disobedience, a law that gave him neither the desire nor the power to obey its commands, and is brought under another law, the law of love, which is not a set of written commandments but an ethical and spiritual dynamic, produced in the heart of the yielded believer by the Holy Spirit, who gives him both the desire and the power to live a life in which the dominating principle is love, God's love, which exercises a stronger and stricter control over the heart and is far more efficient at putting out sin in the life than the legalizers think the thunders of Sinai ever were.

The word *fulfilled* is from *pleroo* which means "to make full," and when used of a task or a course of action, "to fully perform," here, "to fully obey." The verb is in the perfect tense, and the translation could read, "The whole law stands fully obeyed." The idea is not that the whole law is embraced in or summed up in the act of loving one's neighbor as one's self, but that in doing that, one is complying with the whole law and its demands.

Translation. *For the whole law in one utterance stands fully obeyed*: *namely in this, Love your neighbor as you do yourself.*

Verse fifteen. The words *bite* (*dakno*), *devour* (*katesthio*), and *consumed* (*analisko*), were used commonly in classical Greek in connection with wild animals in deadly struggle. The *if* here is from *ei*. That condition was existing in the Galatian churches. Neither the passage itself nor the context tells us in so many words to what this condition of strife was due. But most probably it was strife over matters on which the Judaizers were unsettling them. The words constitute a strong expression of partisan hatred resulting in actions that lead to mutual injury.

By consuming one another, Paul does not mean that they will lose their status as Christians, but that such altercation within the Christian churches will at length if persisted in, destroy the organic community life of the churches.

Translation. *But if you are biting and devouring one another, take heed lest you be consumed by one another.*

> 2. *The subjection of the saint to the personal control of the indwelling Holy Spirit, is the secret of victory over sin and of the living of a life in which divine love is the motivating impulse* (5:16-26).
>
>> a. *The Holy Spirit will suppress the activities of the evil nature as the saint trusts Him to do so, and cooperates with Him in His work of sanctification* (5:16-21).

Verse sixteen. The words "I say then," throw emphasis upon the statement which they introduce. Paul now introduces a statement intended to counteract the erroneous impression held by the Galatians, possibly at the suggestion of the Judaizers, that without the restraining influence of the law, they would fall into sin. Instead of an attempted law obedience in their own strength motivated by the terrors of the law, Paul admonishes them to continue to govern their lives by the inward impulses of the Holy

Spirit. The type of life and the method of living that life which he here speaks of, Paul had already commended to them in 5:5, in the words "For we through the Spirit wait for the hope of righteousness." Thus, the secret of victory over sin is found, not in attempted obedience to a law that has been abrogated, but in subjection to a divine Person, the Holy Spirit, who at the moment the sinner places his faith in the Lord Jesus, takes up His permanent residence in his being for the purpose of ministering to his spiritual needs.

The word *walk* is from *peripateo* which means literally "to walk about," but when used in a connection like this, refers to the act of conducting one's self, or ordering one's manner of life or behavior. The word *lust* is from *epithumia* which refers to a strong desire, impulse, or passion, the context indicating whether it is a good or an evil one. The word *flesh* refers here to the totally depraved nature of the person, the power of which is broken when the believer is saved. Therefore, the lusts of the flesh refer to the evil desires, impulses, and passions that are constantly arising from the evil nature as smoke rises from a chimney. The evil nature is not eradicated. Its power over the believer is broken, and the believer need not obey it. But it is there, constantly attempting to control the believer as it did before salvation wrought its work in his being.

The word *fulfill* is from *teleo* which here means "to bring to fulfillment in action." The verb is future, and is preceded by two negatives. Two negatives in Greek do not, as in English, make a positive assertion. They strengthen the negation. We have here an emphatic promissory future. It does not express a command, but gives a strong assurance that if the believer depends upon the Spirit to give him both the desire and the power to do the will of God, he will not bring to fulfillment in action, the evil impulses of the fallen nature, but will be able to resist and conquer them.

We must be careful to notice that Paul puts upon the *believer,* the responsibility of refusing to obey the behests of the evil nature by conducting himself in the power of the Holy Spirit, and under His control. The will of the person has been liberated from the enslavement to sin which it experienced before salvation, and is free now to choose the right and refuse the wrong. The Holy Spirit has been given him as the Agent to counteract the evil nature, *but He does that for the saint when that saint puts himself under His control, and by an act of his free will, says a point-blank positive NO to sin. In other words, there must be a cooperation of the saint with the Holy Spirit in His work of sanctifying the life.* The Holy Spirit is not a perpetual motion machine which operates automatically in the life of the believer. He is a divine Person waiting to be depended upon for His ministry, and expecting the saint to cooperate with Him in it. Thus the choice lies with the believer as to whether he is going to yield to the Holy Spirit or obey the evil nature. The Spirit is always there to give him victory over that nature as the saint says a point-blank NO to sin and at the same time trusts the Spirit to give him victory over it.[26]

Translation. *But I say, Through the instrumentality of the Spirit habitually order your manner of life, and you will in no wise execute the passionate desire of the flesh.*

Verse seventeen. The word *against* is from *kata,* the root meaning of which is *down,* and which thus has the idea of suppression. The words "are contrary" are from *antikeimai* which means "to lie opposite to," hence "to oppose, withstand." The words "the one to the other" are from *allelos,* a reciprocal pronoun in Greek. Thus, there is a reciprocity on the part of the flesh and Spirit. Each reciprocates the antagonism which the one holds for the other. The translation is as follows: *For the flesh constantly has a strong desire to suppress the Spirit, and the Spirit constantly has a strong desire to suppress the flesh. And these are entrenched in an attitude of mutual opposition to one another, so that you may not do the things that you desire to do.*

When the flesh presses hard upon the believer with its evil behests, the Holy Spirit is there to oppose the flesh and give the believer victory over it, in order that the believer will not obey the flesh, and thus sin. When the Holy Spirit places a course of

---

26. *Riches,* pp. 96-103, 111-114.

conduct upon the heart of the believer, the flesh opposes the Spirit in an effort to prevent the believer from obeying the Spirit. The purpose of each is to prevent the believer from doing what the other moves him to do. The choice lies with the saint. He must develop the habit of keeping his eyes fixed on the Lord Jesus and his trust in the Holy Spirit. The more he says NO to sin, the easier it is to say NO, until it becomes a habit. The more he says YES to the Lord Jesus, the easier it is to say YES, until that becomes a habit.

The will of the believer is absolutely free from the compelling power of the evil nature. If he obeys the latter, it is because he chooses to do so. But the Holy Spirit has given the believer a new nature, the divine nature. And the sweet influences of that nature are constantly permeating the activities of the believer's will as the believer keeps himself yielded to the Spirit. In that way, the Spirit keeps on suppressing the activities of the evil nature and any control which it might attempt to exert over the saint.

Verse eighteen. The Galatian Christians had up to the time of the Judaizers' entry into their churches, lived their Christian lives in dependence upon the Holy Spirit, in accordance with the teaching of the apostle Paul. The power of the sinful nature had been broken, the divine nature had been implanted, and the Spirit had entered their hearts to take up His permanent residence. The conflict spoken of in verse 17 had been going on in them, and the result had been that they were living victorious lives over sin (4:19). But now a new factor had entered, the law, and with it, their dependence upon self effort to obey that law. The Galatians were still trying to live Christian lives, but they were going about it in the wrong way, with the result that they were failing. The entrance of these new factors meant that the Spirit had no opportunity to minister to their spiritual lives. The mechanical set-up of spiritual machinery which God had installed, had become ineffective by reason of the monkey-wrench of self-dependence which the Galatians had thrown into it.

Paul here presents to them a third way of life, distinct from that of a person under law, and also from that of a person who, because he is not under the restraining influences of law anymore, thinks that that leaves him without restraint of any kind, and thus yields to the impulses of the evil nature. That third way is not a middle road between these two, but a highway above them. It is a highway of freedom from statutes and from the sinful nature, a highway which is a faith way, a dependence upon the Spirit.

The exhortation is therefore, to be led by the Spirit. The assurance is given those who do so, that they will not be living their lives on the principle of legalism. The Spirit and the law are here contrasted, and are shown to be methods of living a Christian life that are diametrically opposed to one another. *The law is not only no safeguard against the flesh, but rather provokes it to more sin. Therefore, the believer who would renounce the flesh, must renounce the law also. Thus, the flesh and the law are closely allied, whereas the flesh and the Spirit are diametrically opposed to one another.*

Again, the law finds nothing to condemn in the life of the person who is led by the Spirit, for that person checks every wrong desire which is brought to him by the evil nature, and so he fulfills the law. This is the blessed moral freedom of the person who is led by the Spirit. He is in such a condition of moral and spiritual life that the law has no power to censure, condemn, nor punish him. This is the true moral freedom from the law to which Paul refers (Rom. 8:1-4).

Translation. *But if you are being led by the Spirit, you are not under law.*

Verse nineteen. Paul's purpose in enumerating the various manifestations of the evil nature, is to enforce the exhortation of verse 13 to the effect that the Galatian Christians are not to use their liberty from the law as a base of operations from which to cater to the flesh, but instead, are to rule their lives by love. Such a catalogue of sins would act as a repellent and thus cause them to turn away from sin. The word *manifest* is from *phaneros*, which means "open, evident" so that anyone may see, hence, "well-known." Paul appeals to their common knowledge. It is as if Paul said to the Galatians, "You have a clearly defined standard by which to decide whether you are being led by the Holy Spirit or by the flesh. Each is known by its peculiar works or fruits."

The word *works* is from *ergon*. It is probably to be understood as active rather than passive, as referring to the deeds rather than to the products of the evil nature. The word *uncleanness* is from *akatharsia* which is used in the New Testament of sensual impurity. *Lasciviousness* is from *aselgeia* which refers to lawless insolence and wanton caprice. The word is not limited to impurities of the flesh. It speaks of one who acknowledges no restraints, who dares whatever his caprice and wanton petulance may suggest. It refers to one who has an insolent contempt for public opinion, and shamelessly outrages public decency. *Demosthenes*, making mention of the blow which Meidias had given him, characterizes it as in keeping with the well-known *aselgeia* of the man.

The word *which* is from *hatina*, the relative and indefinite pronouns combined into one word, the combination having a qualitative function. That is, all the works of the flesh are not here enumerated, but enough of them are, so that the reader may be able to form an estimate of their character. The word *adultery* is not in the best Greek texts, hence the reason for its omission in the translation.

Translation. *Now the works of the flesh are well-known, works of such a nature as for example, fornication, uncleanness, wantonness.*

Verse twenty. Idolatry is from *eidololatreia*, a word which denotes worship of an image or of the god represented by it. *Witchcraft* is from *pharmakia*, which word speaks in general of the use of drugs, whether helpfully by a physician, or harmfully by someone whose purpose it is to inflict injury, hence, in the sense of poisoning. Aristotle, Polybius, and the LXX use the word of witchcraft, since witches used drugs. In Isaiah 47:9, it is a synonym of the word *epaiode* which means *enchantment*. In the LXX, the word is uniformly used in a bad sense, of the witchcraft or enchantments of the Egyptians (Ex. 7:11, 22), the Canaanites (Wisdom 12:4), and the Babylonians (Isa. 47:9, 12). It is used in the New Testament to refer to sorceries (Rev. 9:21). In the present passage, the reference is to witchcraft, sorcery, magic art, without special reference to the use of drugs.

Hatred is from *echthra*, the opposite of love. It speaks of enmity and hostility in whatever form manifested. The word is plural in the Greek text. *Variance* is from *eris* which refers to contention, strife, fighting, discord, quarreling, wrangling. *Emulations* is from *zelos* which refers to jealousy, the unfriendly feeling excited by another's possession of good, and to envy, the eager desire for possession created by the spectacle of another's possessions. *Wrath* is from *thumos* which refers here to passionate outbursts of anger or hostile feeling. *Strife* is from *eritheia* which means "self-seeking, selfishness, factiousness." *Seditions* is from *dichostasia* which speaks of dissensions and divisions. *Heresies* is from *hairesis*. The verb of the same stem means "the act of taking, of choosing." Thus the noun means "that which is chosen." It can refer therefore to a chosen course of thought or action, hence one's chosen opinion, and according to the context, an opinion varying from the true exposition of the Word of God, in the latter sense, heresy. It also refers to a body of men separating themselves from others and following their own tenets. The word could have incidental reference to the Judaizers and their teachings.

Translation. *Idolatry, witchcraft, enmities, strife, jealousy, angers, self-seekings, divisions, factions.*

Verse twenty one. Revellings is from *komos* which refers to "a nocturnal and riotous procession of half-drunken and frolicsome fellows who after supper parade through the streets with torches and music in honor of Bacchus or some other deity, and sing and play before the houses of their male and female friends; hence used generally of feasts and drinking parties that are protracted till late at night and indulge in revelry" (*Thayer*).

The word *do* is from *prasso* which means "to do, to practice." It is durative in action, thus speaking of the habitual practice of such things, which indicates the character of the individual. The Word of God bases its estimation of a person's character, not upon his infrequent, out-of-the-ordinary actions, but upon his habitual ones, which latter form a true indication of character. Such people, the apostle says, shall not inherit the kingdom of God.

Translation. *Envyings, drunkenness, carousings, and the things of such a nature which are like these things, respecting which things I am telling you beforehand even as I told you in advance, that those who are in the habit of practicing things of that nature, shall not inherit the kingdom of God.*

> b. The Holy Spirit will produce His own fruit in the life of the saint as the latter trusts Him to do that, and cooperates with Him in His work of sanctification (5:22-26).

Verses twenty two and twenty three. These verses continue the exhortation of Paul to the Galatians, not to make their liberty from the law a base of operations from which to serve the flesh, but rather to live their Christian lives motivated by divine love. As the repulsiveness of the works of the flesh would deter the Galatians from yielding to the evil nature, so the attractiveness of the fruit of the Spirit would influence them to yield themselves to the Spirit. The word *but* is from *de,* is slightly adversative, and introduces the subject of the fruit of the Spirit as a contrast and in antithesis to the works of the flesh.

The choice of *fruit* here instead of *works* is due probably to the conception of the Christian experience as the product of a new and divine life implanted in the saint. In 5:25, Paul speaks of the fact that the Christian lives in the Spirit, that is, derives his spiritual life from the indwelling Spirit, which spiritual life is the motivating force producing the fruit of the Spirit. The word *fruit* is singular, which fact serves to show that all of the elements of character spoken of in these verses are a unity, making for a well-rounded and complete Christian life.

The particular word for *love* here is *agape*. It is the love that God is (I John 4:16), produced in the heart of the yielded believer by the Holy Spirit (Rom. 5:5; Gal. 5:22), its chief ingredient, self-sacrifice for the benefit of the one loved (John 3:16), its constituent elements listed in I Corinthians 13. *Joy* is from *chara,* which is used most frequently in the New Testament of joy that has a spiritual basis, for instance, "joy of the Holy Ghost" (I Thess. 1:6). *Peace* here is not the peace with God which we have in justification, but the peace of God in our hearts, and can be defined as *tranquility of mind based on the consciousness of a right relation to God.* It is from *eirene* which in its verb form means "to bind together." Thus, Christ Jesus through the blood of His Cross binds together that which was separated by human sin, the sinner who puts his faith in the Lord Jesus, and God.

Longsuffering is from *makrothumia* which speaks of the steadfastness of the soul under provocation. It includes the idea of forbearance and patient endurance of wrong under ill-treatment, without anger or thought of revenge. *Gentleness* is from *chrestotes* which refers to benignity and kindness, a quality that should pervade and penetrate the whole nature, mellowing in it all that is harsh and austere. *Goodness* is from *agathosune.* The word refers to that quality in a man who is ruled by and aims at what is good, namely, the quality of moral worth. It is so used in Ephesians 5:9, II Thessalonians 1:11, and Romans 15:14. *Faith* is from *pistis* which does not refer here to faith exercised by the saint, but to faithfulness and fidelity as produced in the life of the yielded Christian by the Holy Spirit.

Meekness is from *prautes,* which was used in Greek writers to refer to the qualities of mildness, gentleness, and meekness in dealing with others. *Temperance* is from *egkrateia* which means "possessing power, strong, having mastery or possession of, continent, self-controlled." It is used in I Corinthians 7:9 of the control of sexual desire. In I Corinthians 9:25, it is used of the control of the athlete over his body and its desires, during the period in which he is in training for the stadium athletic games.[27] The word thus refers to the mastery of one's own desires and impulses. The word does not in itself refer to the control of any particular or specific desire or impulse. The context in which it is found will indicate what particular desire or impulse is meant, if a particular one is referred to.

---

27. Bypaths, pp. 52-54.

The words "against such there is no law," are an understatement of Paul's thought in the premises, and are for the purpose of rhetorical effect. This mild assertion to the effect that there is no law against such things, has the effect of an emphatic statement that these things fully meet the demands of the law.

Translation. *But the fruit of the Spirit is love, joy, peace, longsuffering, kindness, goodness, faithfulness, meekness, self-control. Against such things there is no law.*

Verse twenty four. Christians crucified the evil nature with its affections and lusts, in the sense that when they put their faith in the Lord Jesus as Saviour, they received the actual benefits of their identification with Christ in His death on the Cross, which benefits were only potential at the time He was crucified. The Christian's identification with Christ in His death, resulted in the breaking of the power of the sinful nature over the life. This victory over sin which the Lord Jesus procured for us at the Cross, is made actual and operative in our lives as we yield to the Holy Spirit and trust Him for that victory. It is the Holy Spirit's ministry that applies the salvation from the power of the sinful nature which God the Son procured at the Cross for us. Thus the Holy Spirit has a two-fold ministry in the saint, that of making actually operative in the life of the Christian, the victory over sin which the Lord Jesus procured for us at the Cross, and that of producing in the Christian's experience, His fruit. But this He is only able to do in a full and rich measure as the saint puts himself definitely under subjection to the Spirit. This initial act of faith in the Lord Jesus which resulted in the crucifixion (putting to death) of the affections and lusts of the totally depraved nature, is followed during the life of that Christian, by the free action of his liberated will in counting himself as having died to (having been separated from the power of) the evil nature with the result that he says NO to sin and stops yielding himself and his members to sin.[28]

The word *affections* is from *pathema* which means " a disposition, an impulse, a propensity, a passion." The word *lusts* is from *epithumos* which means "a desire, a craving, a longing."

---
28. Treasures, pp. 94-99.

The former word is passive in its significance, speaking of the innate forces resident in the evil nature. The latter word is active in its nature, speaking of these forces reaching out to find expression in the gratification of these desires.

Translation. *And they who belong to Christ Jesus, crucified the flesh with its dispositions and cravings once for all.*

Verse twenty five. The word *Spirit* is dative of reference. The word *if* is the conditional particle of a fulfilled condition. That is, "in view of the fact" or "seeing that" we live with reference to the Spirit. The Galatians were living with reference to the Spirit in the sense that the new divine life resident in their beings, was supplied by the Spirit. Now, Paul says, " in view of the fact that you Galatians have a new life principle operating in your beings, then walk by the Spirit." The word *walk* is from *stoicheo* which means "to walk in a straight line, to conduct one's self (rightly)."

Thus, the exhortation is to the Galatians who have divine life resident in their beings, to conduct themselves under the guidance, impulses, and energy of that life. Here we have the free will of the Christian and his responsibility to live the highest type of Christian life, and the grace of God which will make that possible. *The responsibility of the saint is to desire to live a Christlike life, to depend upon the Holy Spirit for the power to live that life, and to step out on faith and live that life. This fulfilled, will bring all the infinite resources of grace to the aid of the saint, and put in operation all the activities of the Spirit in his behalf.*

Translation. *In view of the fact that we are being sustained in (spiritual) life by the Spirit, by means of the Spirit let us go on ordering our conduct.*

Verse twenty six. The words, "vain glory" are from *kenodoxos* which means, "having a conceit of possessing a rightful claim to honor." It speaks of that state of mind which is contrasted to the state of mind which seeks God's glory. There were two classes of Christians in the Galatian churches. One class thought that they had attained to freedom in the absolute sense, freedom from any restraint whatsoever. These were in danger of turning liberty into license. This class took pride in their fancied liberty from all restraint. The other class was composed of the more scrupulous and timid brethren. The former class would be tempted to dare the latter group to do things which the law forbids, insinuating that they were afraid to do them. The former class thus would be guilty of vain glory, empty pride, provoking the latter group to do things which it did not think right.

On the other hand, the latter group would be tempted to regard the spurious liberty of the former class as something to be desired, and thus would envy them their liberty, wishing that they felt the same way about their freedom. It is like the case of the strong Christian and the weak one who has scruples. Romans 14:1-15:3 and I Corinthians 8 deal with this subject. The strong Christian should bear the infirmities of the weak, Paul said. This would be the cure for the situation in the Galatian churches.

Translation. Let us stop becoming vain-glorious, provoking one another, envying one another.

III. *The Galatian saints who have not been enticed away from grace by the wiles of the Judaizers, and who therefore are still living Spirit-controlled lives, are exhorted to restore their brethren who have been led astray, back to the life under grace* (6:1-5).

Verse one. This verse is closely connected with the contents of chapter 5. In the latter chapter, two methods of determining conduct and following out that determination with the appropriate action, are presented. One is in dependence upon the Holy Spirit for the supply of both the desire and the power to do the will of God. This method results in a life in which the fruit of the Spirit is evident. The other method is that of putting one's self under law, and by self effort attempting to obey that law. This results in a defeated life full of sin, for the law gives neither the desire nor the power to obey it, and on the other hand, uses the evil nature as a means by which to bring sin into the life, since the evil nature is aroused to active rebellion by the very presence of the law. Those Galatians who were adopting the latter method in conformity to the teaching of the Judaizers, were finding that sin was creeping into their lives. Since they were most earnestly zealous of living a life of victory over sin, and in conformity to the ethical teachings of the New Testament dispensation, the presence of sin in their lives was a source of surprise to them. They found that sin often appeared in their lives before they were conscious of its presence, and at a time when they were not at all conscious of harboring any sinful desire. They were in about the same position as Paul before he knew of the delivering power of the Holy Spirit, when he said, "I am carnal, sold under sin. For that which I do, I do not understand: for what I would (the good), I do not; but what I hate (the evil), that I do.... For to will is present with me: but how to perform that which is good I find not.... For the good that I would I do not: but the evil which I would not, that I do" (Rom. 7:14, 15, 18b, 19). That is exactly the predicament which many Christians are in today, since they do not have an intelligent understanding of the ministry of the Holy Spirit, and the needful and correct adjustment of the Christian to the Spirit, and are consequently depending upon self effort to obey the ethics of the Pauline epistles, or the legal enactments of the Mosaic law. Deprived therefore of the ministry of the Holy Spirit, the lives of the Galatians were an easy prey to the Tempter of men's souls, and he was working havoc amongst them.

That brings us to a consideration of the word translated "overtaken." The context which we have presented will help us in determining the meaning of the word as it is used here. The word is *prolambano*. It has the following meanings: "to anticipate, to forecast, to overtake, to come upon, to take unawares." Two of our Greek authorities, *Lightfoot* and *Alford,* think that the reference here is to the act of a Christian detecting a fellow-Christian in the commission of a sin, thus catching him unawares in it, and establishing by that means the fact of the sin. Four, *Burton, Vincent, Expositors,* and *Meyer* think that it refers to the Christian himself being overtaken by the sin before he is aware that he has done wrong. *Robertson* merely defines the word without interpreting it. The context rules in favor of the opinion of the four. *Vincent* says, "surprised by the fault itself." *Expositors* says, "His surprise in the very act."

The word *fault* is from *paraptoma*. The word means "a fall beside, a false step, a blunder, a failure to achieve." It is in antithesis to *walk* in 5:25, which latter word (*stoicheo*) means "to walk in a straight line." The word in the papyri means "a slip or lapse," rather than "a wilful sin." Paul used the word *parabasis* in 3:19 (*transgressions*), where he spoke of sin as a wilful stepping beyond the limits imposed by law. There he was speaking of the ministry of the Mosaic law in showing unsaved man that sin was not only the following of evil impulses, but that it was the violation of the laws of God. Here the apostle is speaking of the case of a Christian, who while desiring wholeheartedly to do the right, yet does the wrong because he is not availing himself of the God-appointed method of living the Christian life. His sin is not therefore the deliberate violation of God's will and His Word, but a lapse into sin through a helplessness to prevent it, a helplessness however self-imposed in this case, for the Galatians had had the ministry of the Spirit taught to them by the apostle who has recorded his failure as a Christian when living under law, in Romans 7, and the way of victory which he afterwards found, in Romans 6 and 8.

The spiritual among the Galatians, namely, those who were still living their lives in dependence upon the Spirit, are exhorted to restore those Galatians who had abandoned that method for the one taught by the Judaizers. The word *restore* is from *katartizo*. This word has the following meanings: "to repair, to restore to a former good condition, to prepare, to fit out, to equip." It is used of reconciling factions, of setting bones, of putting a dislocated limb into place, of mending nets, of manning a fleet, of supplying an army with provisions. It is used by Paul usually in a metaphorical sense of setting a person to rights, of bringing him into line. Those Galatians who had not abandoned their dependence upon the Holy Spirit, now are asked by Paul to set those Galatians right who had been seized unawares by sin because they had deprived themselves of the ministry of the Spirit. The primary thing that they needed to be set right about was

Verse three. If one has the conceited idea that he is morally and spiritually superior to what he actually is, this tends to make him unwilling to take the burden of responsibility for the restoration of a sinning fellow-saint. A Christian of that character, so far from fulfilling the law of the Christ, is deceiving himself as to his true status in the Christian experience.

Translation. *For if anyone thinks himself to be something when he is nothing, he is deceiving himself.*

Verse four. Here is the case of the self-deceived man of the previous verse, who boasts of his own superiority when he compares himself with the Christian brother who has fallen into sin. He has a ground for boasting only in respect to his much-vaunted superiority to his inferior brother. But the man who puts himself to the test without comparing himself with others, bases his appraisal of himself on an absolute rather than a relative foundation, upon himself alone.

Prove is from *dokimazo* which means "to put to the test for the purpose of approving." The exhortation is therefore to Christians not to form an estimate of themselves by comparing themselves with others, but to put themselves to the test to find out what there is in their characters and in their lives which would merit approval. The word *rejoicing* is from *kauchema* which means "that of which one glories or can glory, matter or ground of glorying." The word is not connected with the word *glory* (*doxa*) which is used of God's glory. It means *glory* in the sense of exultation, self-congratulation. It does not however have the idea of an excessive or unjustified estimate of one's self that the English word *boasting* has.

Translation. *But his own work let each one put to the test and thus approve, and then with respect to himself alone will he have a ground for glorying, and not with respect to the other one (with whom he had compared himself).*

Verse five. The word *burden* in 6:2 is *baros*, and in this verse, *phortion.* While these words have their distinctive meaning in the secular usage of the early centuries, and while synonyms in juxtaposition should usually be carefully distinguished, yet we cannot draw a fine distinction between these two words in this passage. There is no use burdening the English reader with the various meanings of the two words, since they would have no bearing upon our study. In 6:2 the apostle exhorts the Galatian saints to bear the burdens of their fellow saints, namely, to assume the responsibility of giving that saint spiritual aid in case he has allowed sin to come into his experience. Here he exhorts the saints to bear their own burdens. This is doubtless an intentional paradoxical antithesis on the part of the apostle. It is the Christian who knows that he has a burden of his own, namely, a susceptibility to certain sins, and who has fallen himself, who is willing to bear his neighbor's burden. Again, when each man's self-examination reveals infirmities of his own, even though they may not be the same as those of his neighbors, he will not claim moral and spiritual superiority to others. Furthermore, each saint should bear his own burden in the sense that he must recognize his personal responsibilities towards God and man. He is responsible for the kind of life he lives. Again, when he sees his own failings, he will have no inclination to compare himself with others. The word *own* is from *idios*, which means "pertaining to one's self, one's own as compared to that which is another's." It speaks of personal, private, unique possession.

Translation. *For each shall bear his own private burden.*

IV. *The Galatian saints who have deserted grace for law, are exhorted to put themselves under the ministry of the teachers who led them into grace, and are warned that if they do not, they will reap a harvest of corruption* (6:6-10).

Verse six. The word *taught* is from *katecheo* which refers to the act of giving instruction, usually orally. It refers to oral teaching here, because that was the only form of instruction then in existence in the churches. The person referred to has received oral instruction in the Word of God. The word *communicate* means "to share, to be a partner in a thing with a person," here "to hold fellowship with another person." That in which the person holds fellowship with another is designated by the context. The one who is taught should hold fellowship with his teachers in all good things. What the good things are is defined by the context. In verses 1-4, Paul exhorts the Spirit-filled saints in the Galatian churches to take upon themselves the responsibility of restoring to the right method of living a Christian life, those who had put themselves under law, and also that of restoring to fellowship with the Lord Jesus, these saints who had sin in their lives because of their lapse from sanctifying grace. In neither of these evil things, namely, the act of deserting grace for law, and that of committing an act of sin, could the Spirit-filled Galatians hold fellowship with those who had followed the Judaizers. Nor could these spiritual Galatians hold fellowship with the Judaizers, for the latter were not teaching the Word of God nor were they ministering good things to them. Therefore, the good things of verse 6 refer to spiritual things, since they are compared to the evil things just spoken of.

Now, the Judaizers had precipitated a situation in the Galatian churches in which those who followed their teaching broke fellowship with the true teachers of the Word. Paul is exhorting these to resume their fellowship with their former teachers and share with them in the blessing of grace which their teachers were enjoying. The exhortation is that the disciple should make common cause with the teacher in everything that is morally good and which promotes salvation. This breach that had interposed itself between some of the Galatians and their teachers who had taught them grace (Paul included), could not but interfere with their moral and spiritual life. The Galatians' growth in grace was largely dependent upon their attending the means of grace afforded by the presence and ministry of the teachers in their midst who had taught them grace. Furthermore, the work of the churches was hindered by this disruption. The disciple is not to leave the sphere of the morally good as Paul taught it, to the teacher alone, and go off to the Judaizers. He is to work in common with his teachers and so promote the spiritual life of the churches.

The interpretation that makes the one taught assume the responsibility for the financial welfare of his teacher is not possible in this instance of the use of the word *koinoneo*. This is the word

Paul uses in Philippians 4:15, where he speaks of the obligation of the one taught to make the financial needs of his teacher his own, thus sharing with his teacher his earthly goods inasmuch as the teacher has shared with him his heavenly blessings. But Paul does not use it so here, and for the following reasons: *First,* the context which speaks both of the evil (6:1-5) and the morally good (6:9, 10), is against the interpretation that financial support is in the apostle's mind here. *Second,* the context defines the good things as being of a spiritual, not a material nature. *Third,* it would be the height of folly for Paul to inject such a delicate subject as the pocket book of the saint (delicate in some circles) into the already discordant atmosphere of the Galatian churches, especially when the whole trouble revolved around heretical teaching and not around the finances of the churches. *Fourth,* if Paul were exhorting the saints to contribute financially to the support of their former teachers, the Judaizers would be quick to say that the apostle was attempting to win the Galatian saints back to grace for financial reasons, since he himself was one of their former teachers. One of the favorite methods of attack adopted by the enemies of Paul was to charge him with commercializing his ministry. He would not lay himself open to this charge by such an unwise act as in the present circumstances exhorting the Galatians to resume their financial responsibility with reference to the material needs of their former teachers.

Translation. *Moreover, let the one who is being taught the Word, constantly be holding fellowship with the one who is teaching in all good things.*

Verse seven. In verse 6, the apostle exhorts the Galatians to continue to hold fellowship with their teachers who taught them grace, the implication being that they were not availing themselves of their ministry because they were going over to the Judaizers and their teachings. In this verse, Paul tells the Galatians that they must not think that it is not a matter of importance whether their fellowship be with their former teachers who taught them the truth, or with the Judaizers who were teaching them error.

He says to them, "Stop deceiving yourselves, God is not mocked." The construction is present imperative in a prohibition, which forbids the continuance of an action already going on. The Galatians were saying to themselves already, "It is not important which teachers we listen to, Paul and his associates, or the teachers of the law." Thus, they were already deceiving themselves, and leading themselves astray.

The words *is mocked* come from *mukterizo*. The word means "to turn up the nose, to ridicule, to ignore, to sneer." The word when used rhetorically, referred to the betrayal of covert ill-will and contempt by cynical gestures in spite of fair words. It implies an outward avowal of respect neutralized by an indirect expression of contempt. The thought which Paul wishes to press home to the Galatians is that it is vain to think that one can outwit God by reaping a harvest different from that which a person has sown. The figure of sowing and reaping used for conduct and its results is a frequent one. In the Greek classics we have, "For he that is furnished the seed, is responsible for what grows." Paul therefore warns the Galatians against being led astray by the Judaizers, and reminds them that they cannot outwit God in doing so, for it will lead to disaster in their lives and chastening from the hand of God.

Translation. *Stop leading yourselves astray. God is not being outwitted and evaded. For whatever a man is in the habit of sowing, this also will he reap.*

Verse eight. The word *to* in the expressions, "to the flesh" and "to the Spirit," is from *eis*, which latter is not used here in its local use, for instance where seed is dropped into the ground, but in the sense of "with a view to." Sowing with a view to the evil nature refers to the act of a person choosing those courses of conduct that will gratify the cravings of the totally depraved nature. In this context, these words refer to the Galatians who in following the teachings of the Judaizers, catered to the desires of the evil nature. All false systems of religion are so adjusted that they appeal to the fallen nature of man, satisfying his religious instinct for worship, while at the same time allowing him to go on in his sin. The teachings of the Judaizers catered to the fallen natures of the Galatians in that they made no demand for the necessity of regeneration nor for faith in an atoning sacrifice that paid for sin. In addition to that, their teachings stressed a salvation-by-works religion, which glorifies man, not God, and which allows him to go on in his sin while seeking to buy the favor of God by his so-called good works. This could only lead, Paul says, to corruption in their lives. From our study of the contents of chapter 5 we have seen that such corruption was already starting in the lives of the Galatians.

The one who sows with a view to the Spirit, that is, the one who chooses his courses of conduct with a view to fulfilling the wishes of the Holy Spirit, is the Christian who reaps the blessings of the eternal life which God has given him.

Translation. *Because the one who sows with a view to his own flesh, from his flesh as a source shall reap corruption. But the one who sows with a view to the Spirit, from the Spirit as a source shall reap life eternal.*

Verse nine. In verse 8, Paul exhorts the Galatians to govern their lives with a view to the Spirit's control over them. Now, he exhorts them not to become weary in that course of action. The words "be weary," are from *egkakeo* which was used of husbandmen who are tempted to slacken their exertions by reason of the weariness caused by prolonged effort. The word *faint* is from *ekluo* which was used of reapers overcome by heat and toil. The word means "to relax effort, to become exhausted physically." The incentive to keep on working was, that at the right time they would gather the harvest.

Translation. *Let us not slacken our exertions by reason of the weariness that comes with prolonged effort in habitually doing that which is good. For in a season which in its character is appropriate, we shall reap if we do not become enfeebled through exhaustion, and faint.*

Verse ten. The word *opportunity* is from *kairos*, the same word being used in verse 9 where it is translated *season*. Here it means *opportunity* in the sense of a seasonable time, an appropriate time to do something. The word *have* is from *echo,* a present subjunctive, the apparatus giving a present indicative as a rejected reading. It is hortatory in its usage, namely, "let us be having" a seasonable time. The exhortation is not merely to do good to others when the opportunity presents itself, but to look for opportunities to do good to others. The word *do* is from *ergazomai,* which word emphasizes the process of an action, carrying with this the ideas of continuity and repetition. It means "to labor, to be active, to perform," with the idea of continued exertion being included.

The word *good* is preceded by the article. It is not merely what may be good in character as judged by anybody's standards, but the good spoken of in the context, good which is the product of the work of the Holy Spirit through the saint. The word *unto* is from *pros* which combines the sense of direction with that of active relation to. None of us lives to himself as an isolated unit among his fellowmen. We are bound together in a racial group in which we have certain obligations to them.

The word *household* acquired in a connection like the one in this verse, the general sense of pertaining or belonging. The definite article precedes the word *faith.* The expression refers to those who belong to the Faith, the Christian Faith.

Translation. *So then, in like manner, let us be having opportunity, let us be working that which is good to all, but especially to those of the household of the Faith.*

V. Paul's final warning against the Judaizers and his closing words. (6:11-18).

Verse eleven. Now comes a most pathetic appeal from the great apostle. He says, *Ye see with what large letters I wrote to you with my own hand.* Paul was in the habit of dictating his epistles to an amanuensis, writing the concluding words himself, and signing his name. Tertius, for instance, was the secretary who wrote the letter to the Romans as Paul dictated it to him (Rom. 16:22). These two things, the concluding words in his own handwriting and his signature, constituted the evidence that he was the author of the letter (II Thess. 3:17; I Cor. 16:21;

Col. 4:18). There had been a case of forgery where someone had written a letter to the Thessalonian church to the effect that the Great Tribulation was upon them, and had signed Paul's name (II Thess. 2:1, 2).

A word about the large letters in which Paul wrote. There were two styles of Greek writing, the literary uncial which consisted of inch-high letters formed singly and with no connection with other letters, and the cursive, using smaller letters in a running hand, joined together. According to Sir Frederic Kenyon, there were four classes of workmanship in the style of the manuscripts of the first century. *First,* there was the work of a thoroughly good professional scribe. *Second,* there was the work of a good ordinary professional hand. *Third,* there was the work of an educated man not a professional scribe, writing a careful copy of a literary hand. *Fourth,* there was the running hand of common every day writing. Paul dictated his epistles to Tertius, Sosthenes, Timothy, and Silvanus. These were educated men, but not professional scribes. Therefore their writing would be that of the educated amateur. It is the opinion of Kenyon that Paul's epistles were written in the cursive, that is, in small letters, joined together in a running hand. That means that if Kenyon is right, the original manuscripts of the Pauline epistles were in the cursive style of writing. He states it as his opinion also that if Paul dictated the Galatian letter, the dictated portion would be in the small cursive letters, and the part he wrote in his own handwriting, in uncial or inch-high letters.

Scholars are in disagreement regarding the question as to whether Paul wrote the entire epistle with his own hand in inch-high letters, or only the conclusion. The writer is frank to say that he has rejected the opinion of six of the seven authorities which he has studied throughout this epistle, and has accepted that of Alford to the effect that Paul wrote the entire letter in uncial Greek letters rather than only the conclusion. *Alford's opinion is based upon solid ground, Greek grammar.* The aorist tense in the indicative mode in Greek refers to a past action. It was a courtesy extended by the writer to the reader in closing his letter, to look upon it as the reader would, as a past event, and he used the epistolary aorist for this purpose. The writing of the letter was a present fact to the writer before he closed the letter. Nevertheless he looked upon it while using this aorist verb in the closing portion of the letter as a past event, thus placing himself at the perspective of the reader when the latter would receive it. Zahn in his *Introduction to the New Testament* also holds the view of Alford that Paul wrote the entire letter with his own hand. Zahn makes the point that the epistolary aorist is never used, at least in the New Testament, to refer to something which the writer is about to write. He says that Paul is looking back upon the letter which is just being closed. Alford makes a sharp point when he calls attention to II Thessalonians 3:17 where Paul writes, "The salutation of Paul with mine own hand, which is the token in every epistle, so I write." The words "I write," are in the present tense. They refer here clearly to the concluding words of the letter only. Alford asks the question to the effect that if Paul had written only the concluding portion of Galatians, would he not have used the present tense as in the Thessalonian letter? He says that he does not see how it is possible to avoid the inference that these words in Galatians 6:11 apply to the whole epistle.

The next question is regarding the reason why Paul wrote in large inch-high letters. The writer again desires the reader to know that in this question he has rejected the opinion of six of the authorities he has consulted and has followed Expositor's Greek Testament. Paul had contracted an oriental eye disease called ophthalmia, which not only gave him a repulsive appearance, but rendered him almost totally blind. It was therefore necessary for him to write in letters large enough so that with his darkened vision he could see what he was doing. But why did Paul write the entire letter himself? He could have dictated it to a secretary. The answer is found in the fact that he wanted to have as personal a touch with the Galatians as possible under the circumstances. In 4:20 he had expressed the wish that he were personally present with them. The character of the letter and the circumstances in the Galatian churches made it inadvisable to send a dictated letter. Paul wished to give his letter the highest possible personal character. We cannot know with what pain and difficulty, with his own hand, and in the large letters his impaired vision compelled him to use, Paul wrote this letter. And now he appeals to the tender hearts of the Galatians. They would remember the afflicted apostle, and how graciously they had received him. He appeals to their tender emotions, not to forsake him, their suffering, self-sacrificing teacher. It is a most pathetic note.

Translation. *Ye see with what large letters I wrote to you with my own hand.*

Verse twelve. The Judaizers were attempting to escape persecution from their Jewish brethren who had rejected Jesus as Messiah and as the Lamb of God who takes away the sin of the world, those who had held aloof from the visible Christian church and were maintaining the Temple ritual. They had identified themselves with the visible church, and therefore were looked upon by their Jewish brethren outside of the church as having joined an organization that taught grace as against law. They however did not believe in grace, but instead, in works as a means of salvation. Now, to keep from being persecuted by the rest of Israel on the charge that they had embraced salvation through faith in the Cross of Christ, they were attempting to foist circumcision and finally the entire Mosaic economy upon the Gentiles in the Church, for the Cross of the Lord Jesus had put an end to the Mosaic law, and anyone who accepted the law, rejected the Cross. The Judaizers wished to remain in good standing with the Jewish community. Of course, back of the activities of the Judaizers was that sinister being, Satan, archenemy of God and the Church, seeking to destroy the latter.

The words *the cross* are used by Paul here to refer to the whole doctrine of salvation through the crucifixion of the Lord Jesus viewed as the substitutionary atonement for sin. The words "to make a fair show," are from *euprosopeo* which is made up of the words *eu* meaning *well*, and *prosopon*, *face*, thus "to present a good looking face." This is its literal meaning. The lexicon definition is, "to please, to make a fair show." The Judaizers desired to appear pleasing to their Jewish brethren who still clung to the Temple sacrifices and refused to have anything to do with the visible Christian church, pleasing in a doctrinal way. To do this, they would have to show them that they still held to the Mosaic economy. The easiest way to do this was to attempt to put the Gentiles in the Church under the law. Circumcision was the point at issue at the time. The Galatians had already succumbed to the Jewish feasts. More of the law would be added as opportunity presented itself.

Translation. *As many as desire to make a good outward appearance in the sphere of the flesh, these are trying to compel you to receive circumcision, their only motive being that they might not be persecuted by reason of the cross of Christ.*

Verse thirteen. The Judaizers not only attempted to impose circumcision on the Gentiles in order to placate their Jewish brethren outside of the Church and win their confidence and regard in spite of the fact that they were identified with a body of people who taught grace, but also to cover up their own laxity in fulfilling all the requirements of the Mosaic law. In their act of forcing, if possible, circumcision upon the Gentiles, they would cover themselves with glory in the eyes of their Jewish brethren, and demonstrate to them how zealous they were of the law after all.

Translation. *For not even those who are circumcised, themselves are keeping the law, but they desire you to be circumcised in order that in your flesh they may glory.*

Verse fourteen. In contrast to the Judaizers who gloried in human attainment and self effort as a means of salvation, Paul boasted in the Cross of Christ. The world of which Paul speaks here is the world Paul knew before he was saved, the world of Philippians 3:4-6, his Israelitish ancestry, his Pharisaic traditions, his zeal for the law, in short, the world in which he had lived. To all this now he was dead. He had been separated from it by the Cross of the Lord Jesus. It had no more appeal to him nor influence upon him.

GREEK NEW TESTAMENT 179

Translation. *For, as for me, far be it from me to be glorying, except in the cross of our Lord Jesus Christ, through whom to me the world stands crucified, and I to the world.*

Verse fifteen. In this verse, Paul gives his reason for glorying in the Cross of Christ. It is because, while circumcision is of no avail to the Jew, nor the lack of circumcision of any avail to the Gentile, yet the Cross has power to make of believing Jew and Gentile a new creation which results in a radical transformation of character.

Translation. *For[29] neither circumcision is anything, nor uncircumcision, but a new creation.*

Verse sixteen. The word *walk* is from *stoicheo* which means "to direct one's life, to order one's conduct." *Rule* is from *kanon* which here means "a principle." The principle here is the Cross and all that goes with it in the New Testament economy, including of course the ministry of the Holy Spirit which is so much in evidence in this last section of Galatians. Those therefore, who order their lives by the Holy Spirit's control, constitute the true Israel of God, not the Jews who have the name of Israel but are only children of Abraham after the flesh. The Greek word for "and" also has the meaning of "even" in some contexts. We translate here, "even the Israel of God" as identifying those who "walk according to this rule."

Translation. *"And as many as by this rule are ordering their conduct, peace be upon them, and mercy, even upon the Israel of God.*

Verses seventeen and eighteen. "As for the rest" is from *tou loipou,* a genitive of time, "henceforth." The word *marks* is from *stigma.* The word had various uses. Slaves in the Phrygian temples with which the Galatians were familiar, were attached for life to the service of the temple, and were branded with the name of the deity. The name was the *stigma* or mark. Slaves and soldiers bore branded upon their bodies the names of their masters and commanding generals. The marks (*stigma*) of the Lord Jesus were the scars that were caused by the scourgings, the

---
29. The words "in Christ Jesus" are a rejected reading.

Roman rods, and the stoning at Lystra which Paul had received. The word *bear* is from *bastazo* which means "to bear what is burdensome." Paul's body, marked by the assaults made upon his person, must often have been wracked with pain. Paul was a man old before his time, partly by reason of the sufferings he endured at the hands of his enemies, the Judaizers. He asks that such a situation as obtained in the Galatian churches be not repeated. The sufferings which he endured for the sake of the Lord Jesus and the gospel of grace, should deter the Galatians from adding more sufferings to the already full complement of suffering which the apostle had already borne, by again precipitating a situation like the present one which severely taxed the energies of the aged apostle as he sought to save his beloved Galatians, and the Christian Church for that matter, from a spiritual catastrophe, the evil effects of which would work havoc for the cause of Christ.

Translation. *Henceforth, let no man give me trouble, for I bear branded the marks of the Lord Jesus in my body. The grace of our Lord Jesus Christ be with your spirit, brethren. Amen.*

4

The Complete Letter in a Fuller Translation

Now, that you have studied the Galatian letter verse by verse, may we suggest that you read it through in order that you might have a comprehensive grasp of it in its broad perspective. *Read it through at a single sitting. Do this repeatedly.* The fuller translation of each verse has been given with the exegesis of its contents. But in order that the reader might obtain a comprehensive grasp of Paul's letter, we have added it in its entirety.

TRANSLATION

Paul an apostle, not from man (as an ultimate source), nor even through the intermediate agency of a man, but through the direct agency of Jesus Christ and God the Father, the One who raised Him out from among the dead, and all the brethren with me, to the assemblies of Galatia. Grace to you and peace from God the Father and the Lord Jesus Christ, who gave Himself in behalf of our sins so that He might rescue us out from this present pernicious age, according to the will of our God and Father, to whom be the glory for ever and ever. Amen.

I am marvelling that in such a manner suddenly, you are becoming of another mind and are deserting from Him who called you in the sphere of Christ's grace to a message of good news diametrically opposed to the gospel, which message is not another gospel of the same kind. Only there are certain ones who are troubling your minds, and are desiring to pervert the gospel of Christ. In fact, even if we or a messenger from heaven preach a gospel to you which goes beyond that which we preached to you, let him be accursed. Even as we have said on a previous occasion, indeed, now again I am saying, If as is the case, anyone preaches a gospel to you which goes beyond that which ye took so eagerly and hospitably to your hearts, let him be accursed. For, am I at this present moment seeking to win the favor of men rather than the approval of God? Or, am I making it my business to be constantly pleasing men? If I still were pleasing men, in that case Christ's bondslave I would not be.

For I make known to you, brethren, the gospel which was announced as good news by me, that it is not as to its nature, human. For as for myself, neither did I receive it directly from man, nor was I taught it, but I received it through a revelation given me by Jesus Christ.

For you heard of my manner of life aforetime in Judaism, that beyond measure I kept on continuously persecuting the Church of God and continuously bringing destruction upon it, and I was constantly blazing a pioneer path, outstripping in Judaism many of my own age in my race, being more exceedingly zealous of my ancestral traditions.

But when it was the good pleasure of the One who set me apart before I was born, and called me by His grace, to give me an inward revelation of His Son in order that I might proclaim Him as glad tidings among the Gentiles, immediately I did not put myself in communication with flesh and blood for the purpose of consultation; neither did I go up to Jerusalem to those who were apostles before me, but I went away into Arabia, and again returned to Damascus.

Then after three years I went up to Jerusalem to become acquainted with Kephas, and remained with him fifteen days, but another of the apostles I did not see except James the brother of our Lord. But the things which I am writing to you, behold, before the face of God, I am not lying. Then I went into the regions of Syria and Cilicia, but I remained personally unknown to the churches of Judaea which are in Christ. Indeed, they only kept on hearing, The one who used to persecute us at one time, is now announcing the glad tidings of the faith which at one time he was ravaging. And they were continually glorifying God (for that which they found) in me.

Then after the space of fourteen years, again I went up to Jerusalem accompanied by Barnabas, having taken along also Titus. And I went up in accordance with a revelation. And I laid before them for their consideration, the gospel which I am preaching among the Gentiles, but privately to those of recognized eminence, lest by any means I should be running or had run in vain. But not even Titus who was with me, although he was a Gentile, was compelled to be circumcised. Now it was because of the false brethren who had been surreptitiously brought in, those of such a character that they sneaked in for the purpose of spying out our liberty which we are having in Christ Jesus, with the expectation of reducing us to abject slavery, to whom not even for an hour did we yield with reference to the particular voluntary submission (demanded), in order that the truth of the gospel might abide for you. But to be something from (at the hands of) those who were of repute, whatever they were aforetime, is of no importance to me. God accepts not man's person. For those who were of repute imposed nothing on me. But on the contrary, when they saw that I had been entrusted with (the responsibility of preaching) the gospel to the uncircumcised as Peter with (the responsibility of preaching) the gospel to the circumcised, for He who worked effectively for Peter with respect to (his) apostolate to the circumcision, also worked effectively for me with respect to the Gentiles, and having come to perceive the grace which was given to me, James, and Kephas, and John, those who in reputation were looked upon as pillars, gave to me and Barnabas the right hands of fellowship, to the end that we should preach the gospel to the Gentiles and they themselves to the circumcision. Only that we should keep on remembering the poor, which very thing I have made a diligent and eager effort to do.

But when Kephas came to Antioch, to his face I opposed him, because he stood condemned. For before certain from James came, with the Gentiles it was his habit to eat meals. But when they came, he began gradually to draw himself back, and began slowly to effect a final separation, fearing those of the circumcision. And the rest of the Jews also played the hypocrite jointly *with him, so that even Barnabas was swept along with their hypocrisy. But when I saw that they were not pursuing a straightforward course in relation to the truth of the gospel, I said to Kephas in the presence of everybody, If you being a Jew, habitually are living after the manner of the Gentiles, and not after that of the Jews, how is it that you are compelling the Gentiles to live after the Jewish manner? As for us, we are Jews by nature, and not sinners of Gentile origin, and knowing that a man is not justified by law works but only through faith in Christ Jesus, we also placed our trust in Christ Jesus, in order that we might be justified by faith in Christ and not by law works, because by law works there shall no flesh be justified. But if, as is the case, while seeking to be justified in Christ, we (Jews) ourselves also were found to be sinners, is Christ therefore a promoter of sin? Away with the thought; for if the things I tear down, these again I build up, I exhibit myself as a transgressor; for, as for myself, I through the intermediate agency of the law died to the law, in order that I might live with respect to God. With Christ I have been crucified, and it is no longer I who live, but there lives in me Christ. And that life which now I live in the sphere of the flesh, by faith I live it, which faith is in the Son of God who loved me and gave Himself on my behalf. I do not thwart the efficacy of the grace of God. For if through law comes righteousness, then Christ died without a cause.*

O, unreflecting Galatians, who bewitched you, before whose eyes Jesus Christ was placarded publicly as the Crucified One? This only am I desiring to learn from you. By means of law works did you receive the Spirit or by means of the message which proclaims faith? Are you so unreflecting? Having begun by means of the Spirit, now are you being brought to maturity by the flesh? So many things did you suffer in vain? If indeed they really were in vain? Therefore, the One who is constantly supplying the Spirit to you in bountiful measure, and constantly working miracles among you, by means of law works is He doing these things, or by means of the message which proclaims faith?

Just as Abraham believed God, and his act of faith was credited to him, resulting in (his) righteousness. Ye perceive, therefore, that those who are of faith, these are sons of Abraham. And the scripture forseeing that on a basis of faith God justifies the Gentiles, announced the gospel beforehand to Abraham, namely, All the Gentiles shall be blessed in you. So that those who are believing ones are being blessed in company with believing Abraham.

For as many as are of the works of the law, are under curse. For it stands written, Cursed is every one who is not remaining constantly in all things which stand written in the book of the law in order to do them. But that in a sphere of law no one is being justified in the sight of God is clear, because, The righteous man shall live by means of faith. And the law is not of faith; but the one who has done them, shall live in them. Christ delivered us by the payment of ransom from the curse of the law by becoming a curse in behalf of us, because it stands written, Accursed is every one who is suspended upon a tree, in order that to the Gentiles the blessing of Abraham might come in Jesus Christ, in order that the promise of the Spirit we (Jew and Gentile) might receive through faith.

Brethren, what I have to say is in accordance with common human practice. Even though it be a man's covenant, when it has finally been ratified, no man annuls it nor adds stipulations to it. Now to Abraham were made the promises, and to his seed. He does not say, And to the seeds, as in respect to many (seeds), but in respect to one (seed), and to your seed who is Christ. This now is what I mean. A covenant previously established by God, the law, which came after four hundred and thirty years, does not render void, with the result that the promise becomes inoperative, for if the inheritance is from law (as a method of divine dealing), no longer is it from promise (as a method of divine dealing). But to Abraham through the intermediate instrumentality of promise God has in grace freely bestowed it.

What is then the significance of the law? For the sake of transgressions it was added, until there should come the Seed to whom the promise was made, having been promulgated by angels through the instrumentality of the hand of a mediator. Now, the mediator is not (a go-between representing the interests) of one (individual), but God is one (individual). Is therefore the law against the promises of God? God forbid. For if a law had been given which was able to impart life, righteousness in that case would have been from the law. But the scripture shut up all under sin, in order that the promise on the ground of faith in Jesus Christ might be given to those who believe. But before the aforementioned faith came, under law we were constantly being guarded, being shut up with a view to the faith about to be revealed.

So that the law became our guardian until Christ, in order that on the grounds of faith we might be justified, but (this) faith having come, no longer are we under the guardian, for all of you are God's sons through faith, in Christ Jesus, for as many as were introduced into (a mystical union with) Christ, put on Christ. There is neither Jew nor Greek, there is neither slave nor free, there is neither male nor female. For ye are all one in Christ Jesus. And since ye are Christ's, then are ye Abraham's seed, heirs according to the promise.

Now I say, that as long as the heir is in his minority, he does not differ one bit from a slave, even though he is owner of all, but is under guardians and stewards until the time previously fixed by his father. In like manner, we also, when we were in our minority, were in a permanent state of servitude under the rudimentary first principles of mankind. But when there came the fulness of the time, God sent off His Son, woman born, made subject to law, in order that He might deliver those under law, in order that we might receive the placing as adult sons. And because ye are sons, God sent forth the Spirit of His Son into your hearts crying Abba, my Father. So that no longer are you a slave but a son, and since (you are) a son, (you are) also an heir through God.

But at that time in fact, not knowing God, ye were in a slave's bondage to the gods which are not gods by nature. But now having come to know God, indeed rather having become known by God, how is it possible that you are turning back again to the weak and beggarly rudimentary principles to which ye are bent on again being in bondage? Days ye are scrupulously and *religiously observing, and months, and seasons, and years. I am afraid about you lest perhaps in vain I have labored to the point of exhaustion for you.*

Become as I am, because I also became as you were, brethren, I am beseeching you. Ye had done me no wrong. But ye know that because of an infirmity of the flesh, I preached the gospel to you on the occasion of my first visit. And the temptation to which ye were subjected and which was in my flesh, ye did not loathe nor utterly despise, but as a messenger of God ye received me, as Christ Jesus. Where is therefore your (spiritually) prosperous state? For I bear witness to you that if it had been possible, you would have dug out your own eyes and would have given them to me. So then I have become your enemy because I am telling you the truth. They are zealously paying you court, but not honestly, desiring to isolate you in order that you might be paying court to them. But it is good to be zealously courted in a good thing at all times, and not only when I am present with you, my born ones, concerning whom I am again striving with intense effort and anguish until Christ be outwardly expressed in you. Moreover, I was wishing that I were present with you at this very moment, and could thus change my tone, because I am perplexed about you.

Tell me, ye that are bent upon being under law, are ye not hearing the law? For it stands written, Abraham had two sons, one from the maidservant and one from the freewoman. But on the one hand, the son of the maidservant was one born in the ordinary course of nature. On the other hand, the son of the freewoman was one born through the promise. Which class of things is allegorical. For these are two covenants, one from Mount Sinai, begetting bondage, which is as to its nature classed as Hagar. Now this Hagar is Mount Sinai in Arabia, and corresponds to the Jerusalem which now is, for she is in bondage with her children. But the Jerusalem which is above is free, which is our Mother. For it stands written, Rejoice, barren (woman) who does not bear. Break forth and cry, you who do not travail, because more are the children of the desolate than of the one who has an husband. And, as for you, brethren, after the manner of Isaac are ye children of promise. But just as then he who was born according to the flesh was constantly persecuting him who was born according to the Spirit, so also now. But what does the Scripture say? Throw out the maidservant and her son. For the son of the maidservant shall by no means inherit with the son of the freewoman. Therefore, brethren, we are children not of a maidservant, but of the freewoman.

For this aforementioned freedom Christ set you free. Keep on standing firm therefore and stop being held in again by a yoke of bondage. Behold, I, Paul, am saying to you that if you go on (persist in) being circumcised, Christ will be advantageous to you in not even one thing, and I solemnly affirm again to every man who receives circumcision, that he is under obligation to do the whole law. You are without effect from Christ, such of you as in the sphere of the law are seeking your justification. You have lost your hold upon grace. For, as for us, through the agency of the Spirit, on the ground of faith, a hoped-for righteousness we are eagerly awaiting, for in Christ Jesus, neither circumcision is of any power nor uncircumcision, but faith coming to effective expression through love. You were running well. Who cut in on you and thus hindered you from obeying the truth? This persuasion is not from the One who calls you. A little leaven is leavening the whole lump. As for myself, I have come to a settled confidence in the Lord with respect to you, namely, that you will take no other view than this. But the one who troubles you shall bear his judgment, whoever he is. And I, brethren, if I am still preaching circumcision, why am I in spite of this fact being persecuted? Then the stumbling-block of the Cross has been done away with. I would that they who are upsetting you, would even have themselves mutilated.

For, as for you, upon the basis of freedom you were called, brethren. Only do not turn your liberty into a base of operations for the flesh, but through love keep on constantly serving one another, for the whole law in one utterance stands fully obeyed: namely in this, Love your neighbor as you do yourself. But if you are biting and devouring one another, take heed lest you be consumed by one another.

But I say, Through the instrumentality of the Spirit habitually order your manner of life, and you will in no wise execute the passionate desire of the flesh, for the flesh constantly has a strong desire to suppress the Spirit, and the Spirit constantly has a strong desire to suppress the flesh. And these are entrenched in an attitude of mutual opposition to one another, so that you may not do the things that you desire to do. But if you are being led by the Spirit, you are not under law. Now the works of the flesh are well-known, works of such a nature as for example, fornication, uncleanness, wantonness, idolatry, witchcraft, enmities, strife, jealousy, angers, self-seekings, divisions, factions, envyings, drunkenness, carousings, and the things of such a nature which are like these things, respecting which things I am telling you beforehand even as I told you in advance, that those who are in the habit of practicing things of that nature shall not inherit the kingdom of God.

But the fruit of the Spirit is love, joy, peace, longsuffering, kindness, goodness, faithfulness, meekness, self-control. Against such things there is no law. And they who belong to Christ Jesus, crucified the flesh with its dispositions and cravings once for all. In view of the fact that we are being sustained in (spiritual) life by the Spirit, by means of the Spirit let us go on ordering our conduct. Let us stop becoming vain-glorious, provoking one another, envying one another.

Brethren, if however, a man be overtaken (by sin) in a certain false step, as for you who are spiritual ones, be restoring such an one in a spirit of meekness, taking heed to yourself, lest you also be tempted. One another's burdens be ye constantly bearing, and thus you will fully satisfy the requirements of the law of the Christ. For if anyone thinks himself to be something when he is nothing, he is deceiving himself. But his own work let each one put to the test and thus approve, and then with respect to himself alone will he have a ground for glorying, and not with respect to the other one (with whom he had compared himself), for each shall bear his own private burden.

Moreover, let the one who is being taught the Word, constantly be holding fellowship with the one who is teaching in all good things. Stop leading yourselves astray. God is not being outwitted and evaded. For whatever a man is in the habit of sowing, this also will he reap; because the one who sows with a view to his own flesh, from his flesh as a source shall reap corruption, but the one who sows with a view to the Spirit, from the Spirit as a source shall reap life eternal. Let us not slacken our exertions by reason of the weariness that comes with prolonged effort in habitually doing that which is good. For in a season which in its character is appropriate, we shall reap if we do not become enfeebled through exhaustion, and faint. So then, in like manner, let us be having opportunity, let us be working that which is good to all, but especially to those of the household of the Faith.

Ye see with what large letters I wrote to you with my own hand. As many as desire to make a good outward appearance in the sphere of the flesh, these are trying to compel you to receive circumcision, their only motive being that they might not be persecuted by reason of the cross of Christ, for not even those who are circumcised themselves are keeping the law, but they desire you to be circumcised in order that in your flesh they may glory. For, as for me, far be it from me to be glorying, except in the cross of our Lord Jesus Christ, through whom to me the world stands crucified, and I to the world. For neither circumcision is anything, nor uncircumcision, but a new creation. And as many as by this rule are ordering their conduct, peace be upon them, and mercy, even upon the Israel of God. Henceforth, let no man give me trouble, for I bear branded the marks of the Lord Jesus in my body. The grace of our Lord Jesus Christ be with your spirit, brethren. Amen.

INDEX

	Page		Page
Galatians 1:1	28	Galatians 2:21	82
Galatians 1:2	31	Galatians 3:1	83
Galatians 1:3	32	Galatians 3:2	85
Galatians 1:4	32	Galatians 3:3	85
Galatians 1:5	35	Galatians 3:4	86
Galatians 1:6	35	Galatians 3:5	87
Galatians 1:7	35	Galatians 3:6	88
Galatians 1:8	39	**Galatians 3:7**	92
Galatians 1:9	40	Galatians 3:8	92
Galatians 1:10	42	Galatians 3:9	93
Galatians 1:11	43	Galatians 3:10	94
Galatians 1:12	44	Galatians 3:11	95
Galatians 1:13	46	Galatians 3:12	96
Galatians 1:14	47	Galatians 3:13	96
Galatians 1:15	49	Galatians 3:14	98
Galatians 1:16	49	Galatians 3:15	99
Galatians 1:17	51	Galatians 3:16	101
Galatians 1:18	53	Galatians 3:17	101
Galatians 1:19	53	Galatians 3:18	102
Galatians 1:20	54	Galatians 3:19	103
Galatians 1:21	54	Galatians 3:20	106
Galatians 1:22	55	Galatians 3:21	107
Galatians 1:23	55	Galatians 3:22	108
Galatians 1:24	56	Galatians 3:23	108
Galatians 2:1	56	Galatians 3:24	110
Galatians 2:2	58	Galatians 3:25	110
Galatians 2:3	60	Galatians 3:26	111
Galatians 2:4	60	Galatians 3:27	111
Galatians 2:5	62	Galatians 3:28	112
Galatians 2:6	62	Galatians 3:29	112
Galatians 2:7	63	Galatians 4:1	112
Galatians 2:8	65	Galatians 4:2	112
Galatians 2:9	65	Galatians 4:3	113
Galatians 2:10	67	Galatians 4:4	114
Galatians 2:11	68	Galatians 4:5	115
Galatians 2:12	70	Galatians 4:6	116
Galatians 2:13	72	Galatians 4:7	117
Galatians 2:14	74	Galatians 4:8	118
Galatians 2:15	76	Galatians 4:9	118
Galatians 2:16	77	Galatians 4:10	122
Galatians 2:17	**78**	Galatians 4:11	123
Galatians 2:18	79	Galatians 4:12	123
Galatians 2:19	80	Galatians 4:13	124
Galatians 2:20	81	Galatians 4:14	125

INDEX—Continued

	Page		Page
Galatians 4:15	126	Galatians 5:14	150
Galatians 4:16	127	Galatians 5:15	152
Galatians 4:17	127	Galatians 5:16	152
Galatians 4:18	128	Galatians 5:17	154
Galatians 4:19	128	Galatians 5:18	155
Galatians 4:20	130	Galatians 5:19	156
Galatians 4:21	132	Galatians 5:20	157
Galatians 4:22	132	Galatians 5:21	158
Galatians 4:23	132	Galatians 5:22	159
Galatians 4:24	133	Galatians 5:23	159
Galatians 4:25	133	Galatians 5:24	161
Galatians 4:26	133	Galatians 5:25	162
Galatians 4:27	134	Galatians 5:26	162
Galatians 4:28	134	Galatians 6:1	163
Galatians 4:29	134	Galatians 6:2	167
Galatians 4:30	134	Galatians 6:3	168
Galatians 4:31	135	Galatians 6:4	168
Galatians 5:1	136	Galatians 6:5	168
Galatians 5:2	137	Galatians 6:6	169
Galatians 5:3	138	Galatians 6:7	171
Galatians 5:4	140	Galatians 6:8	172
Galatians 5:5	141	Galatians 6:9	173
Galatians 5:6	142	Galatians 6:10	173
Galatians 5:7	142	Galatians 6:11	174
Galatians 5:8	143	Galatians 6:12	177
Galatians 5:9	143	Galatians 6:13	178
Galatians 5:10	144	Galatians 6:14	178
Galatians 5:11	145	Galatians 6:15	179
Galatians 5:12	146	Galatians 6:16	179
Galatians 5:13	148	Galatians 6:17	179
		Galatians 6:18	179